WILL THE VAMPIRE PEOPLE PLEASE LEAVE THE LOBBY?

True Adventures in Cult Fandom

AN

ALLYSON BEATRICE

SOURCEBOOKS, INC.
NAPERVILLE, ILLINOIS

Published by Sourcebooks, Inc.
P.O. Box 4410, Naperville, Illinois 60567-4410
(630) 961-3900
Fax: (630) 961-2168
www.sourcebooks.com
ISBN-13: 978-1-4022-0845-4
ISBN-10: 1-4022-0845-6
Library of Congress Cataloging-in-Publication Data is on file with the
publisher.

Printed and bound in the United States of America
VP 10 9 8 7 6 5 4 3 2 1

This whole mess is dedicated to the
following crazy people:

Tim, for crushing my fear under the boot of the writer.
The Vampire People, for a lifetime of great stories.
And to my parents, for everything else (and that's a lot).

Table of Contents:

Acknowledgments:

Many thanks to the following people for their support, good counsel, and in some cases, for allowing me to exploit them for personal gain: Lauren Abramo; ita; Sara Anderson; Jason, Erin, and Gavin Beatrice (plus the littlest one on the way); Jacqui Biscobing; the Bitch Cabal; Michael Boretz; Rebecca Boston; Chris Buchanan; Sarah Bunting; B298 Horology; the Buffistas, Bronzers, and Browncoats; Paula Carlson; Aimee Conat; Drew Dalzell; Jane Espenson; David Fury; Amy Garvey; Deborah Grabien; John Gray; Kat Gullo; the Hillhurst Coffee Bean; Jesse Hergert; Michelle Jensen; Nathan Lundblad; Peter Lynch; Jenny Lynn; Nilly Madar; Brenda Martinez; Laura McCoy; Erin McKean; Kate McKean; Robin Miller; Lee N.; Maria Neve; G & J Orndorff; Amy Pascale; Popgurls; Kristen Reidel; Lori Shiraishi; Maya Stosskopf; Susan Tankersly; Angela Tavares; Stevie Tuszynski; Jillian Venters; Caroline van Oosten de Boer and Simon Fraser at Whedonesque; and Joss Whedon.

And all the people I forgot to put on this list.

Everyday Apocalypses

I haven't given much thought to *Buffy the Vampire Slayer* since the series ended in May 2003. Other people have. There's an annual academic symposium called The Slayage Conference on Buffy the Vampire Slayer. Academics from all over the world come to present papers on a variety of topics centered on the cult show with the odd name.

Here's a sampling of titles from past conferences: "Driving Stakes, Driving Cars: California Car Culture, Sex, and Identity in *Buffy the Vampire Slayer*" by Brett Rogers and Walter Scheidel (Stanford University); "'You Hold Your Gun Like A Sissy Girl': Firearms and Anxious Masculinity in *Buffy the Vampire Slayer*" by Stevie Simkin (King Alfred's College); and

"*Buffy the Vampire Slayer* and the Domestic Church: Re-Visioning Family and the Common Good" by Reid B. Locklin (Boston University).

There's even a treatise floating around the internet on planning for dirty bombs and anthrax-filled envelopes. It's published by a defense think tank, The Center for Strategic and International Studies and it's titled, "Biological Warfare and the *Buffy* Paradigm" by Anthony H. Cordesman. It's a historical critical analysis of the United States' political strategy in the War On Terrah in comparison to the strategies Buffy uses in the War on Vampires. I shit you not.

I think the academics obsessing over *Buffy the Vampire Slayer (BtVS),* tying obscure cultural/socio/historical events to the tiny cult show is weird. Having said that, I realize that I am the unstoppable pot, crashing into the immovable kettle. I had spent thousands of hours discussing the show with my fellow fans. By the time the series ended, I had exhausted my ability to find meaning in the color and style of Buffy's leather pants. After seven years of an obsessive, unhealthy relationship with the wee blonde Chosen One, Buffy and I parted ways. I still love her, my smart, tough, and stylish Wonder Woman with all of her flaws and whining and heroism and poor choices in lovers. We just can't be together anymore.

The reason I look ever-so-hypocritically down my nose at those writing desperate comparative analyses of vampire fashion in relation to the mating habits of snowy owls is because there was a point in my life when I would have taken it all very seriously and argued a well-researched rebuttal, and I feel a sense of pity that these folks are still stuck in a continuous loop of *Buffy* watchage though the show has been off the air for as many years as it was actually worth watching.

I feel vicious, like I'm kicking a one-legged, brain-dead puppy on a feeding tube in Florida. I usually feel fiercely protective of *Buffy* fans, but the thing that crawls up my back and sinks its teeth into my spine about the academic papers is that the authors seem to be taking it all very seriously. It's the antithesis of *BtVS,* and her fandom, to ignore the wink and nudge at the absurdity of the journey. It is a hallmark of historical/critical analysis to compare and contrast absurd combinations of events to make a point. I remember writing a research paper comparing the dim-witted excess and super-ugly fashion choices present in *Saturday Night Fever* to Cold War policies in the '70s. I have no idea what my point was, but I'm sure if I read it now, I'd find it hilarious.

Maybe it's because I was such a mess when I was an avid viewer that I can't watch the show anymore, let alone give it any sort of meaningful critique. Looking back on it, my huge fangurl crush on *BtVS* was just a vehicle to get somewhere else in my life, and once I had made the journey, I sent the show over to the junkyard to be compacted and recycled into something else useful, like Zippo lighters or something.

Buffy wasn't a way for me to gain greater understanding of Firearms and Anxious Masculinity, it was a way for me to gain a better understanding of people and the relationships that can be built upon the tiniest scrap of shared experience. In my case, the scrap was simply the forty-six minutes of television I watched on Tuesday nights.

During the times in my adult life when I've been lonely or frightened, I found solace leaning on the fandom. Those strangers living inside the electric walls of my beat-up Macintosh Performa were like a white-collar geek platoon. My band of brothers pulling me through the shit.

I've always been fascinated by the sense of community and trust I found online. My cyberfamily, scattered all over the planet, have left their fingerprints on just about every aspect of my life, and have brought me more joy than I probably deserve. The real-life people, the *Buffy* fans living in my decade-old Mac, chiseled my life into what it is today. It's the greatest cause of my disconnect from the academic explication of the show. The show, as it turned out, was little more than a very entertaining conduit. Let me explain.

I moved to Los Angeles when I was twenty-seven years old. I was burned out in Boston, working long hours with no sense of direction, and no idea what I wanted to do. I'd wake up crying and not know why. I was a drone bee that woke up one day, tired of carrying buckets of nectar to the queen bee, and decided to go on the lam from a future of condo payments and desperate searches for a hipster husband in Cambridge nightclubs.

The decision to pack everything I owned and start a new life in a new place was made as quickly as a kernel of corn exploding in hot oil. It just happened. I did a mental coin flip, either Los Angeles or Manhattan. Heads: West Coast. Tails: East Coast. The Id quarter came up Washington's profile.

That's how I ended up in Los Angeles, sleeping on a friend's floor for three months while searching for a job and an apartment. It really was just like that. I made the decision to run, quit my job, packed everything in boxes, purchased a one-way ticket, and there I was in L.A., just a handful of weeks later.

The shock of the move sucker-punched me in the face right around Christmas, six weeks after I arrived. Everything was terrifying. In my first month in L.A., while trying to find my way from downtown to Hollywood, I stopped and asked a gas station attendant for directions. He leaned down to my window, gave me some simple instructions for getting home and said, "Honey, you're in East L.A. This is a bad neighborhood. Please lock your door, roll up your window, and don't stop again."

What he didn't know was that I didn't care. I was already scared beyond all reason. My sense of self-worth was in the toilet, and a good carjacking might just be the thing to test my will to live.

I was teetering between packing my car and driving home, or driving up to the Hollywood sign and making a melodramatic leap off the Y. I was the living embodiment of *The Prozac Diaries*. I was a morose, self-involved, boring wreck of a person. And the L.A. weather completely sucked all the moisture from my skin, so I was also flaky and itchy. Mostly I was terribly lonely and desperate to make something of myself. I wanted to be *important*. I wanted to be respected and loved and adored. The problem with wanting those things was that at the time, I wasn't respectable, loveable, or adorable. I was ugly, scared, and mean. I had gone feral.

The whole time that I was slithering blindly through the putrid muck of self-hatred and humiliation the only thing that kept my head from wandering into the oven was the net. I didn't really give a crap about *Buffy* or *Angel* at that point at all. It was just something familiar. The same people having the same conversations about the same television shows. I could write, "I'm scared. I think I made a terrible mistake," and twenty strangers would tell me it was going to be okay, and tell me stories about their own lonely lives, or how they survived cross-country moves. It was the only constant I had, the only thing that looked the same, worked the same.

Firing up my computer and typing the URL for the official *Buffy* message board, The Bronze, into the browser was my security blanket. But it did nothing to reconstitute the shriveled up raisin that my ego had become. I went from a decent position doing desktop publishing in the training department of a law firm in Boston to being unable to get through a temp job interview without blubbering like a toddler denied a Happy Meal prize.

I needed a job, or at least a hobby, to fill the hours of the day I was using to mentally beat the shit out of myself. I chose fandom.

It all started with a party. A gathering of my fellow net sluts. A woman named Kristen, who would later turn out to be one of the most important people in my world, was throwing a bash at the Paramount Studios Commissary. There was to be a Bacchanalian feast of fruit dipped in chocolate on a stone (or was it foam?) gargoyle's platter. Midnight set tours on the Paramount lot. Candelabra. I was in love with the idea and volunteered my time to the event. It cheered me to throw my shoulder into happiness and PUSH. The party turned out to be a great success, ending in a mass of pretty bodies drunkenly asleep on a hotel floor, as all good parties should end. I don't think I stopped being drunk (metaphorically, of course) for a long time. I felt useful, needed. I was dependable. I was trustworthy. I wasn't a blubbering mess for a few weeks. This was boot camp for my depleted ego. I was a broken down excuse for a person, but I was slowly rebuilding by being responsible for something, even if the something was as small as printing nametags.

Here's a brief timeline of the milestones between printing those nametags and getting a book deal to write essays on my strange life-changing road trip through fandom:

January 2000: Kristen introduces me to Kara, a writer for ScoopMe.com, a now defunct webzine dedicated to reviewing cult and 'tween television shows. Due to Kristen's recommendation, I handled the negotiations to place an Emmy Consideration ad in *Daily Variety* on behalf of ScoopMe, called "Give Buffy an Emmy." *Buffy* never got an Emmy.

March 2000: Kristen runs a site called ScoobyGang.com, which houses all the fan sites for the writers of *BtVS* and

Angel. Of all the sites under the ScoobyGang.com banner, three still survive: TimMinear.net, DavidFury.net, and JossWhedon.net. I staged a coup against the editor of DavidFury.net and took over the site. David Fury remains a friend to this day, and as I'm writing this, he's writing for the megahuge FOX show, *24.*

February 2001: Kristen and I, along with a woman named Maya Stosskopf volunteer to plan an arrival mixer and auction for an infamous party called PBP (Posting Board Party). Most of the cast and crews of *BtVS* and *Angel* join about four hundred fans for inappropriate displays of drunken hero worship and raise $20,000 for the Make-A-Wish Foundation.

March 2002: Erin McKean, a senior editor for Oxford University Press drops me an email asking for assistance getting in touch with Joss Whedon. She wanted to query him about writing a foreword to a book called *Slayer Slang,* a study of the *BtVS* lexicon. Joss declines, but David Fury suggests asking Jane Espenson, a *BtVS* writer who happens to have a degree in linguistics. Jane writes the foreword.

December 2002: Joss Whedon and Tim Minear are totally screwed when their new show, *Firefly,* is canceled by

FOX. Kristen and I swear revenge and set out to save the show with a *Variety* ad and a postcard campaign. We fail miserably, but Minear takes pity on us and gives us *Firefly* crew jackets in gratitude.

.

February 2003: Maya Stosskopf and I decide to incorporate, and our little business, Events by Maya & Allyson (EMA), starts to get paid for our mad party skillz.

February 2004: EMA throws a bash to celebrate and say goodbye to *Angel,* which didn't get its contract renewed. EMA gets a little more business over time, doing book release parties for best-selling romance novelist Suzanne Brockmann, charity fundraisers with the cast and crew of *LOST,* and planning some of the events at the Screenwriting Expo in Los Angeles.

April 2004: After a four hour debate about politics, Tim Minear says, "I don't want you to be a secretary anymore. What do you want to do?" I tell him I want to write a book. He says, "So write a book. Just write it. You're good, you have talent. Just write it and we'll figure out how to get you published." So I start to write this book.

January 2005: A character named Allyson Beatrice gets her face ripped off on *The Inside,* another quickly canceled show by Tim Minear. This has nothing to do with anything, I just mention it because it's so cool.

June 2005: I get an email from Erin McKean, who tells me she heard I was writing a book, and wanted to take a peek at what I had written so far. She sends my work to her sister Kate, who is an agent at some big New York literary agency.

July 2005: Kate emails me and tells me she'd like to represent me.

February 2006: This manuscript lands on the desk of an editor named Peter Lynch at a publishing house called Sourcebooks. Peter happens to be editing a book about *LOST* by David Lavery, who mentions me in his book because EMA threw a big *LOST* party the year before. Lavery also happens to be the founder of the Slayage conference I mention at the beginning of this essay. Seren-fucking-dipity.

So that's how it all went down. The invisible text in between the bullets is full of drunken birthday dinners at the Saddle Ranch chop house on Sunset Boulevard, hysterical crying jags in the parking lot at a Denny's, road trips to San Francisco and San Diego, a million pickups and drop-offs at LAX, a handful of weddings, and the birth of my darling nephew. Fandom has been a constant through all of this. Fandom takes care of my cat when I go on vacation. I sit in the waiting room to take fandom home after wisdom teeth removals. Fandom comes to get me at LAX in the middle of the night when my flight is delayed for eight hours and my luggage has been sent to Australia by mistake. I bring Liquid Plummer to fandom when its toilet explodes. Fandom brings me ginger cookies and sits with me on my stoop when I stupidly lock myself out of my apartment. Fandom, friendom, and familydom all run on a gradient line in my brain. There's no hard shift between the "doms"; they just bleed into each other like watercolors on cheap paper.

My fandom/internet story isn't a weird fluke, either. I suspect there are thousands of books unwritten with similar stories. The anecdotes that make up this collection aren't just mine, there are people within them with their own stories to tell. There are people who met their lovers, partners, or spouses online and now have children born of dialup connections. A generation of Internet Babies. I watched as people got their doctorates, passed the bar exam, got divorced, grappled with the death of a parent, left their homes and countries to start a new life. "Watched" is the wrong verb. I watched *Buffy,* and I engaged the fandom. All of their life stories, as well as mine, are documented in Google searches and long-dead websites that drift on the net like ghost ships. This is the true legacy of *Buffy.* She's the Kevin Bacon of the fandom. The Six Degrees of Separation. All my roads lead back to her. I'm running out of clichés, but you understand what I'm saying.

Of all the research papers presented about *Buffy,* the only ones that interest me are the studies of her audience. Nothing she ever did in the seven years she was on television was ever as heroic, interesting, insane, or gracious as the people watching her. Without them, it's difficult to imagine where I'd be. Maybe riding a desk in the home office of a widget factory north of Boston, wearing spectator pumps and bleaching my hair platinum, with a kid in daycare and a bored husband in someone else's bed. Or maybe I'd be in New York living in an even smaller apartment than I do now, scratching by on an assistant's salary and my dad's handouts. Either way, I imagine I'd be lonely and scared most of the time. I can't quite wrap the gray matter around what I'd do if I couldn't turn on my new iMac and find someone to answer me when I call out in the dark. Screw God, all those times when there were three thousand pairs of footprints in the sand, that's when fandom was carrying me. Or walking with me. Occasionally they were tossing me into the surf.

My point is, they're always with me, and I'm grateful. They're the source I'd cite for the last seven years of the *Story of Allyson*. Ibid.

Will the Vampire People Please Leave the Lobby?

On President's Day weekend about five years ago, two hundred fans of *Buffy the Vampire Slayer* flew thousands—and in some cases thousands and thousands—of miles to attend a much storied bash with the cast and crew of the beloved television series. The fans talked to each other all year on the net, but this was the only time they all saw each other in the same place, face to face. It was like a family reunion of sorts.

The oldest, dearest friends in all the world burst into the Holiday Inn lobby and squealed like fourteen-year-old girls with backstage passes for 'N SYNC. There were hugs all around, much laughter, and screams of sheer delight.

The exasperated employees working the lobby's front desk, however, had enough of the glee and bellowed, "WILL THE VAMPIRE PEOPLE PLEASE LEAVE THE LOBBY?"

The Vampire People. Now, keep in mind that this hotel was otherwise empty; it was a desperate weekend in hotel land with no other conferences in town. The Vampire People filled this hotel at a time of year when hotels are barren, creaky, stale vessels of lunchtime infidelities past. Their tourist dollars didn't matter, though, because they were Vampire People.

Vampire People? We knew this was code for: *You are all fucking dorks. If I weren't miserable here at work, I'd be in a bar, kicking your asses, or sticking maxi pads on your backs so me and my cool friends can laugh at you. How dare you be happy in my presence?*

If fandom were middle school, we'd be the ones suffering the wedgies. Or watching our panties being run up the flagpole.

*   *   *

My friend Fay once described the birth of an internet community as such:

Person A: <sheepishly/shamefully> I . . . I kinda like to wear rubber gloves on my head and pretend to be a chicken. Sometimes. Er. For a laugh, you know?

Person B: I do that every weekend.

Person C: I'm wearing a rubber glove on my head *right now* and it's fucking great! Those non-rubber-glove-wearers (henceforth to be called NRGW) don't know what they're missing!

Person A: Yeah!

Person B: Let's set up our own forum at World Crossing.

Fay's observation is balls-on correct. Internet communities coalesce around a common interest, and sometimes a secret shame. From breast cancer survivors to people who have a diaper fetish, a community of people gather to discuss whatever it is that consumes or interests them. If your community revolves around a "dorky" topic, it's difficult to admit to others what you're typing out into the broadband in your spare time. And just like any "real life" or "meatspace" (where the meat that covers our bones tends to gather, like at a café or study hall) conversation, it's socially cool to discuss sports or cell phone features, while it's completely dorky to talk about vampire slayers.

*   *   *

This all occurred to me while standing in line at The Coffee Bean waiting for a large vanilla latte. I like The Coffee

Bean because they don't make me say *venti* instead of large. While I was waiting, a rather *venti* young man walked in and ordered a mocha.

Now, I don't want to get on the size of this man too much, because, hey, I have a few dozen pounds to lose. I just need to create a visual. He was about six foot two, four hundred pounds of pasty white manflesh, and had nasty, matted black hair sticking out of all the wrong places. And he was wearing a Chicago Bulls away-game uniform, including the Air Jordans.

He could not ever, in this universe or any other alternate universe, be mistaken for Michael Jordan. And yet, there he was, wearing MJ's game uniform. No one in The Coffee Bean blinked, or stared, or whispered. No giggles or pointing. No name-calling. Nothing unusual.

Now picture the same guy dressed as, oh, say, Gandalf the Gray from *Lord of the Rings*. Or Legolas, the girlie-looking elf with the heavy metal hair. Someone would call the cops and he'd be admitted for a seventy-two hour evaluation.

Past the age of four, it suddenly becomes unacceptable and weird to dress up as an elf, or fashion a cape out of an old blanket and pretend to "fly" down the sidewalk. It stops being cute at some point. However, it is acceptable for a fifty-two-year-old man to paint a bull's-eye on his giant gut and jiggle it while naked from the waist up in twenty-degree weather behind the goal post at a Packers game, while wearing a giant wedge of cheese on his head. People in traffic watching him walk into the game may point and laugh, but they're laughing with him. It's acceptable. He's a Great Big Fan Displaying Team Spirit! People like me think the painted Packers fan is a jackass, but we wouldn't dare confront him. He's probably drunk and angry about something.

Sci-fi/fantasy fans don't get Super Bowls and playoff games as an excuse to let their hair down and be obnoxious with fannish love; they have conventions and parties. It's pretty much the same concept, but I think we drink better beer.

*   *   *

So how did all of this begin? Every year on Presidents' Day weekend, *Buffy the Vampire Slayer* fans would gather in Los Angeles for the Posting Board Party (PBP). Originally, all the fans came from an online community called The Bronze, the official posting board for the television series.

The Bronze launched in 1997 at Buffy.com, the official website for the WB television show. Internet communities were still just babies, suckling on the teat of corporate cubicle culture. Employees stuffed into tiny boxes like so much veal, starved for human contact, found places like the Well, Usenet, and AOL chat rooms to slack off at work. There they could get in touch with other people, also stuffed into cubicles. The

Bronze was part of the internet community phenomenon, attracting a group of people that sat in tiny cubes where they stared at a glowing computer screen all day, and then went home to the larger cubes of their living rooms to stare at a glowing television set. The next morning, they'd log onto their computers and go to the Bronze to talk about Buffy and try to forget the beige walls that were closing in all around them.

I was such veal. And I loved me some Buffy. I discovered the Bronze in the spring of 2000, just when I hit a wall of monotony at work. A co-worker made the fantastic suggestion that I should think about what I was worth, divide that by what I was being paid, and the difference would be the number of hours I could spend each day doing jack shit at my desk. This gave me 1.7 hours of slack time, if I rounded up . . . and I did. This was more than one full day of work I spent chatting with other people about television shows and life, and arguing about the wisdom of using strangulation as a means to torture a vampire, since, you know, they don't breathe. I chalked it up as "flextime."

It wasn't long before I was completely entrenched in the community, the fandom. It's amazing what it can do for your ego, to be able to shout something into the dark and have a hundred people shout back. It's about being heard. When your life is a series of spreadsheets and cable bills, it's a soul-affirming thing to be able to escape the craptastic cube farm at any time and actually be heard.

I had become one of the Vampire People. And I was in love with all of the other cube dwellers who were using their "flextime" to talk about the little blonde girl and her big stake. I would have purchased a team jersey, had one been available, but the only merchandise options were Buffy lunch boxes and wall calendars.

*   *   *

In my vast experience with the *Buffy the Vampire Slayer* fandom, I've never seen a fan dress up as a vampire. Or a slayer. People not entrenched in fandom often asked me if we got dressed up for the annual party in Los Angeles. I used to say that lots of people did, and I was always disappointed in folks who would show up in jeans and ratty T-shirts. Then I realized that their scrunched-up noses and smirking smiles were really asking if we dressed up like Buffy, not whether we donned cocktail party attire. I don't know how dressing like Buffy would be accomplished without spending a fortune at Prada and Jimmy Choo's. She's always been such a fashion-forward girl. Even the vampires on *Buffy* were decked out in gorgeous leather dusters and Calvin Klein.

It's hard to pick us out of the herd because we don't have swag. It also makes it harder for us to find each other. That's where the internet comes in. It's a sign of geekdom to walk up to Joe-from-accounting at the water cooler and say, "Hey Joe, did you notice that last night's *Buffy* had a shout-out to William S. Burroughs in the third act?" Odds are good that he didn't watch the episode since Buffy was never the sort of ratings darling that a major sporting event is. Joe-from-accounting now knows you're uncool, and will never take you seriously again. So it's safer to just Google and find your fellow fans, cloaked in the anonymity of the net. People use names like "Closet Buffyholic" and "Leather Jacket" just in case the boss or a disapproving family member happens to stumble across the site and sees their insane ramblings about the Shakespearian metaphors in the characterization of a vampire named Angel.

This was all before the price of computers and internet connections dropped enough so that every thirteen-year-old boy in the U.S. and U.K. could suddenly be online after school without parental supervision, trolling the net and calling everyone attempting a ToGGle-FrEe conversation an ASSHAT in ALL CAPS, lol lol OMG. These were the days when the only people with a computer and high-speed connection were those employed by technologically on-top-of things companies and geeks. There were more of Us than there were of Them, and we all wanted to meet each other and hang out, face to face. In an Alpha Wolf world, we were a pack of Omegas, employed as lawyers, programmers, financial analysts, engineers, Web designers, and college professors in between waxing poetic on the deep metaphors present in the television program with the silly name.

Most of us were decidedly Alpha in our chosen professions, in our "real lives." We just all shared a geek hobby. And though there's usually strength in numbers, it was easy for anyone outside the fandom to see us as weak, as dorks. As Vampire People.

Everyone with whom I've spoken who was in the Holiday Inn lobby the night the desk clerk lost his patience told me that the fandom's reaction was to laugh heartily at the branding. I think the reaction came out of the surprise of being caught with their internet pants down. All these people—successful, likeable, attractive—were suddenly called on their collective odd hobby by an outsider. They were all out of the closet.

* * *

I rarely take more than a quick peek outside of the fandom closet. It just seems like there's way too much to explain, and there's no way I can make it sound normal. I dodge the subject because I can't seem to put it all in concise terms without sounding defensive. For years, I always described the friends I've made through fandom to my mom by saying, "Oh,

Nancy is a friend of a friend at work. She's from Malden, you know." I certainly couldn't have told her Nancy was Paula's sister, and I met Paula at a restaurant in Boston after we talked online at a *Buffy the Vampire Slayer* site. She would have had me committed. There's still that odd stigma, years later, that everyone posting on the internet is out to steal your money or your twelve-year-old daughter, and then kill you with an ax.

The Vampire People will often trade stories of talking around how friendships were made online. There's a whole lot of us who had to compare stories of How We Met before going into a job interview or attending a wedding. When people outside the fandom ask, "So how did you all meet each other?" we share glances across the table, silently looking for consensus about how we'll answer. Depending on the amount of wine consumed, we may answer truthfully. Mostly we just say things like, "Oh we're both from Boston," as if everyone in Boston knows everyone else.

It'd be so much easier if we had away-game team jerseys and could say, "We met in the bleachers at a playoff game." There's no ax-murdering associated with the bleachers or the center ice seats. Still, the conversation had at a ballgame over a couple of hours, between cheers, boos, and trips to the snack bar doesn't seem like enough to develop a life-long friendship, does it? I mean, unless you're a season ticket holder sitting next to other season ticket holders, the sense of camaraderie amongst the thousands of people gathered in a stadium is fleeting. It lasts as long as the game. A message board is available for discussion twenty-four hours a day, year-round.

It's been three years since the series finale of *Buffy* aired, and I still have a hard time telling people just how it is that I have a bed in which to sleep in thirty-two states and five countries.

Someday, it'll be socially acceptable to say, "Oh, we can stop in Des Moines for dinner. I know a couple of Vampire People there."

Minearest and Dearest

Tim Minear is heart-achingly sexy, hopelessly addicted to Marlboro Lights, crazy-smart, politically wrong, infuriatingly moral, wickedly irreverent, and talks faster than I do. He's a walking lightning storm; chaotic and exhilarating and a little bit dark.

When I first met Tim, he was a god. Writer, producer, director, god. He produced *Angel,* one of the television shows we in fandom all followed and ruthlessly scrutinized on dozens of message boards across the internet. In my fandom, writers are the rock stars, held in higher regard than actors. Tim is the Darling One, the Writer Everyone Agrees Rocks So Hard That He Actually Doesn't Just Rock—He *Boulders*.

His claim to fame is an uncanny ability to romance an audience into falling deeply in love with a character and then killing the living shit out of said character.

I first met Tim at a party, a charity benefit of sorts where the actors and producers of *Buffy* and *Angel* would show up to hang out and get manhandled by throngs of adoring masses. He was cool and beautiful in a gray suit, and spent time with anyone who walked up to him to sputter adulation. I had sent him one of my favorite books a few months earlier, on a whim. It was a copy of David Sedaris's *Barrel Fever*. I sent it hoping he would adore it as much as I do and that it would at least be fodder for conversation if I ever had the nerve to speak to my television writing hero.

My opportunity to say something witty and magical came while I was outside the party, smoking and shivering on one of those moist and chilly February evenings in L.A., the kind that makes one feel as though one is trapped inside a side of beef in a meat locker.

Tim burst through the door with a couple of fans in tow, chattering and lighting up cigarettes amongst the rock band noise that came roaring out after them.

I listened to the chatter, and glanced sideways, keeping track of the length of Tim's cigarette, and mentally rehearsed what I needed to say before he got down to the filter, crushed the butt underfoot, and melted back into the club noise.

I introduced myself and sputtered, "Did you read that book I sent you (eight months ago)?"

He registered no memory of the gift, just a sort of blank acknowledgment that I existed. He said he had read the book and thanked me for sending it, anyway. Instead of having a magical moment between me and my hero what I had was a verbal fart, and he was polite enough to not wrinkle his nose while being enveloped in the stench of an awkward moment, trying to give me a bit of dignity. I returned to my lonely cigarette, and mentally kicked myself for not being able to say Something Intriguing.

We fans want our heroes to recognize us. We want to be able to connect in some way, to impress upon them that we, too, are special. Or at least more special than all those *other* fans. Some fans send their heroes books for attention. Others put their hands down their heroes' pants. Either way, we want them to like us in that desperate way the smelly kid in school wants the prom queen to see his inner poet and fall in love with him.

Some of us never make that connection and become bitter, writing hate mail late at night about how our heroes have wronged us in some way by not recognizing and remembering each and every one of us. Some of us just get over it and continue plodding through life.

I'm a plodder. The thing about Tim, though, was that he had an inner spark of irreverence mixed with humility and self awareness that made me intuitively believe that I could lend him my heart and he would return it without a scratch.

Tim was a TableTalker, (a member of the *Angel* Table Talk discussion group) at Salon.com. When an episode he penned aired, he'd show up and answer questions, or procrastinate writing by engaging in debate about crate training beagles or fawning over Camille Paglia. Tim was curiously free with his email address. So I wrote to him . . . a lot. He never answered. It was sort of like writing notes to God and shoving them into crumbling sections of the Wailing Wall.

After a while, writing to Tim was like writing in my journal. I'd send him boring stories of co-workers who done me wrong, boys who done me wrong, family who done me wrong. The subject headings for the crappy electronic anecdotes were always something like Journal Entry #527. I have no idea if he ever read them. I've never asked. I'm sure he remembers none of this.

I needed Tim's approval. He was my hero, after all, and if he thought me worthy of his time that would prove that I was cool and interesting. Tim's enormous talent made him special to me, and to about four million other weekly viewers. If he'd just talk to me, I'd be special by proxy. But by coming to the threads at

TableTalk, Tim was also searching for a bit of approval, a stroke to the ego. He had arrived, professionally speaking, but he still sought out that one-on-one attention, the reassurance from strangers. We weren't so different, maybe, my hero and me.

Eventually, Tim emailed me, breaking his silence. I was at work, filing something, or maybe thinking about filing something when the little red flag on the mailbox got excited and pointed heavenward. I clicked the icon and there it was, no subject, just my hero's name in the "from" column. I stared at it for a second, wanting to shake the email box and admire it for a couple of seconds before tearing into it to see what sort of nifty object was inside.

It was just a single, sharp sentence, poking me in the eye from my email account. "Why is the show sexist?"

I had posted something heated the night before at TableTalk about an episode he wrote that I thought was the definitive proof that the show was turning into a manifesto about the weaknesses of women.

I stared at the screen, raised an eyebrow, and went into a crazy-ass, hyperbolic tangent via email. Despite my fury, I was clearly right. Clearly. I completely forgot to have any sense of reverence. I listed out the indisputable evidence proving my point with a perfect balance of logic and passion. I was momentarily not intimidated by my hero.

His emailed reply was a simple, "You're wrong."

Tim was not God. He was Satan. We argued. Neither of us relented. I get an endorphin high from good debate the way a runner gets it from the ten-mile marker, and Tim is fearless with words. We eventually found common ground in a mutual love for Elvis Costello.

The conversation itself was ridiculous, but it was the beginning of my letting go of that neurosis called hero worship that nagged, "Why would anyone so lovely spend any time with an asshole like me?" It's an exercise in self-hatred to wedge myself into a category of being lesser-than because someone else is more famous, more talented, or richer. It's so much easier for me to say, "Tim, you're being a total dick," than to expend energy trying to justify his human foibles in order to maintain the perfect image I created of him. He has no time for sycophants, anyway. His ego isn't a banana in a blender. In Los Angeles, that's rare.

Over the next couple of years, we sparred sporadically via email. He'd lob a hyperbole bomb over the net, I'd go ballistic, and he'd chuckle and admit to pulling my pigtails. He invited me to tag along with a mutual friend on a set visit or two. I tried to save his shows when they got canceled; he sent me crew jackets for Christmas.

Email banter turned to phone banter when he called me to talk himself down from a shitty situation at work. Conversations blurred from what we do to who we are, and suddenly we're becoming friends, and there's mutual comfort, ego stroking, and blunt-force truth. Like any other friendship. We're not so close that we pick each other up at the airport, and it's still a struggle to get him out of the house to hang out, but we're close enough to start spilling our tiniest secrets, playing the trust game.

I once explained the relationship between fans and heroes to him using the dorks and cool kids in high school analogy, and he said, "You're one of the cool kids, you know that?" I think he didn't quite get it, which is part of what makes him precious to me in a non-Gollum way. The deep moat between Fan and Hero seemed so clear to me. The drawbridge over that moat seemed equally as clear to him. As far as he was concerned, I'd been standing on it for a long time.

When I see Tim now at some convention or party, signing autographs and having his picture taken with fans, I no longer worry about saying anything intriguing. I'm still his fan—always will be—but for reasons that have nothing to do with the work he does while sitting at his computer in his pajamas, two showers past what's reasonable in Russia. I can stumble clumsily over words and land on my ass with my foot firmly lodged in my mouth. He's going to forget all about it in fifty-three seconds and will therefore never be able to hold it against me.

He remembers my birthday, that I come from a blue-collar family, that my eyes are brown, and that I really love chopped liver. Tiny details. He can't remember he has to go to jury duty but knows who I voted for in the last election.

We can talk on the phone for three hours at a time, and when I hang up I have that junior-high flutter in my belly, like I've just made out with a cute boy whom I've been crushing on for weeks. Instead of my mouth being swollen and red from saliva chafe, my neck is sore from balancing the phone on my shoulder while I fold laundry or clip coupons. He reads to me, asks my opinion, and then cuts me off mid-thought to tell me he may have a melanoma, is craving mac and cheese, and then passes judgment on campaign finance reform, all in the same sentence. He's like a three-ring circus of non sequiturs, which is a perfect conversational style for someone with my limited attention span.

I once pointed out to him that I'm still just a fan, and since he was getting all David E. Kelly-famous he wouldn't be having so much time to banter with someone of my meager un-Hollywood status.

Tim replied, "Don't get like that with me EVER A-FUCKING-GAIN." From my perspective, I'm not one of the cool kids. I'm disposable in some way. Tim is a good enough friend to not let my warped issues dictate his opinion of me . . . which is usually much higher than my opinion of me. His ALL CAPS reply made me smile at my screen, for he was calling me on my bullshit.

It must be exhausting to have to convince someone that they are, in fact, worthy of your time. And with that, Tim leaped off the pedestal upon which I had placed him, and helped me pack it into the trunk of my car. I returned it to JCPenney, opting for a merchandise credit for a sassy new pair of Mary Janes.

I'm in love with Tim, in an oddly nonsexual way. There's that invisible line drawn between friends, but he's still a sexy genius who can tear my heart out with a good bit of dialogue and I'm still a girl. I don't want to sleep with him, but I hope to bum cigarettes off him until either lung cancer or melanoma kills one of us. Such is the way with the people closest to my heart.

Munchausen's by Internet

The group dynamics of an internet forum aren't so different than in a high school. There are bullies and dorks, the popular clique and the people who are almost invisible.

The internet forum version of being shoved in a locker is being ignored, or having one of the forum's more popular members call you an asshat, troll, or jackhole.

I survived high school by being the Art Chick. I always had a drawing pad under my arm, chronically focused on a sketch. No one bothers you when you're special in some way, either a paraplegic or the kid who plays guitar really well. It makes you valuable to the group as a whole, and you become part of the protected class. Because in case of

Rapture, we may need someone who can draw really great portraits of Axl Rose.

My friend Lisa from the old *Buffy* forum The Bronze says that my special talent on the net is being an "astute observer with the white-hot caustic wit to point out when bullshit stinks." So flattering.

This all brings me to the strange case of Penlind. Penlind was an adjunct professor at Harvard who was married to an archaeologist. She was related to one of the band members of Barenaked Ladies. She and her husband had a gaggle of adopted children with exotic names like Cairo and Djoser. She was bright, well-read, posted intriguing theories about metaphors in fairy tales, and was a genuinely likable soul. She was extra-super special.

The only problem with Penlind was that she was *actually* a single, childless librarian who had been fired from her previous job for stealing computer equipment, and nothing she said was true. This probably wouldn't have been such a huge problem . . . if she hadn't thrown my little internet community into a state of panic when she claimed her infant son was dying of some sort of rare, complex disease I can't remember.

Penlind was certainly bright enough to have been accepted into the community without the bizarre tales of tragedy and romance. Maybe she didn't think her ability to turn a phrase made her special enough to stand out from the hundreds of other people who dropped by to post on the board. Maybe she was just sick and couldn't really control it.

Munchausen's Syndrome, a factitious disorder, is a mental illness named after a famous baron who made up elaborate tales of adventure. The disorder provides much fodder for tired legal procedural television programs. A kid dies from some sort of rare disease, and the plot twist is that mommy actually poisoned the kid with a bathroom deodorizing product so she could gain sympathy, attention, and the rush of being fussed over by police and doctors. That's Munchausen's Syndrome by proxy. People with Munchausen's syndrome routinely harm themselves, or those in their care in order to be the center of attention.

For someone with a factitious disorder, the internet must be an Eden-like playground, ripe with rubes to pluck and suck dry of all sympathy before moving on to the next community of suckers. Penlind was just that sort of leech. And I was just that sort of rube, at least for a little while.

It's embarrassing to admit, but I got suckered. I mean, she was just so fucking normal, at first. She said she became a *Buffy* fan because her husband's name was Riley, one of the character's names on the show. She said she enjoyed watching *Buffy* so much she did a little search on the net to find out more, and stumbled on our message board.

Over the next few weeks, she offered tiny pieces of information about herself, weaved into lovely posts about cultural anthropology, Little Red Riding Hood metaphors, and general chitchat about books and such. She was fitting in well, liked by every clique. Losers and mean girls alike all thought she was sweet and smart.

It didn't take long for the casual dropping of info-crumbs about her life to turn into a steady leak. Over time, she started allowing her "daughter," Cairo, to post on the board. Even though the girl was supposed to be no more than eight years old, she was thoughtful and articulate. I thought that maybe the kid used spell-check. But Penlind explained that she never allowed Cairo to be on the net unsupervised, and so I figured she would correct spelling and grammar as she typed paragraphs into the little white box. It just seemed so reasonable, right? It's odd how one's mind can smooth out the jagged edges of suspicion in order to make something suspect seem so reasonable.

The first incident of tragedy came bursting onto the screen in the form of Cairo being the victim of a racist attack. Penlind's adopted daughter was black, you see. While she was playing with a neighborhood kid, she was told that black girls can never play the hero, because there are no black heroes. The community of bleeding hearts rushed to her cyberside, me included. I emailed Cairo's story to *Buffy* producer David Fury, who posted a sympathetic response . . . and offered to send Cairo a gift.

Penlind's response was one of dramatic gratitude. In reality, she probably had an orgasm worthy of a carton of cigarettes, as dozens and dozens of people rushed to console her over the next few days.

If that had been it, if the drama had subsided, had things settled down into the usual banter, kerfuffle, and day-to-day ramblings no one would have ever been the wiser. But it didn't end there. I assume that once Penlind came down from the attention high she couldn't help but take another hit of that sweet group-sympathy nectar.

Nothing makes people sadder than dead babies, except maybe dead puppies. Afterall, we see dead babies on the news all the time, but dead puppies hit the news only once a year, when the local anti-cruelty society does one of those public euthanasia shows to shock people into spaying and neutering pets by breaking our hearts with cold reality. But dead babies are still pretty high up there on the sympathy meter. If only Penlind had a dying baby . . . that would make everything all about her for a good, long time.

Penlind's dying baby was named Djoser. He had some sort of rare heart condition. Or maybe it was his liver. At any rate, he was all fucked up. And poor Penlind was all alone, since her husband was away on some archaeological survey somewhere in the Middle East. Or maybe Eastern Europe. Could have been East Boston. It doesn't really matter because he was imaginary, anyway.

She didn't just burst out of a wall like the Kool-Aid man with the news, she leaked it slowly over weeks, peppering everyday conversation with small morsels of medical information about the declining health of her imaginary son. As we all expressed our deepening concerns, wee Djoser's weird medical conditions got weirder. I mentioned all of this to one of my dearest friends, Kristen.

Kristen pulled a thumb-sized violin out from behind my ear and played a dirge for the boy. "Sounds like Munchausen's by internet," Kristen deadpanned.

Heartless! Cynical! And correct, of course. Kristen tied a tourniquet on my gushing heart and presented the facts in all their ridiculous glory. As Kristen listed each piece of Penlind's extraordinary life in tight bullet points, I realized that I was a mark for a sympathy junkie. Kristen wasn't smug about any of it, she's just, you know, a hardcore New Yorker. Her soul is protected by a shield of calcified skepticism. I think it's something in the water. Individually, each piece of Penlind's life story seemed plausible. As a whole, she was a cyber-Forrest Gump.

I know some extraordinary people. I have a friend who helped build the arms on the Mars Rovers, for example. I know a linguist often interviewed on NPR, a woman whose father was the Jamaican Ambassador to Russia, and I knew a woman who would field angry phone calls from legendary House Speaker Tip O'Neill when her journalist father would write something shitty about him in the *Boston Globe*.

Extraordinary people cross my path at a regular clip, but what Kristen was pointing out to me was that nothing about Penlind was just plain *ordinary*.

It was as if she had pulled together excerpts from dozens of romance novels and pasted together a life for herself.

So I went back and read through some of Penlind's posts with a doubtful eye. The first thing that leaped out and gave me a charley horse was a long medical post about how she would be taking little "Djoser" to a specialist in Ireland.

I don't mean to get all jingoistic here, but when one lives in the U.S. one doesn't go to Ireland for medical care. Not when the entire city of Boston, the Mayo Clinic, Cedars Sinai, and a plethora of other hospitals are right here with the world's finest medical minds wandering the halls of every ward.

That morning, I sent a tiny post out into the black: "Has anyone here ever met Penlind, or spoken to her on the phone?"

It was an innocent question. I mean, what if I were wrong? But it was a start. Maybe someone had met her or her children, or had spoken to them on the phone. I was actually hoping that this woman was telling the truth and that she was taking her dying baby to Ireland for some odd medical treatment. Maybe if it was a dying puppy I never would have asked.

Almost the second I posted the inquiry, AOL cheerfully chimed in to tell me, "You've got mail!"

And the mail kept coming. My email box was filling with people whispering, "I don't believe anything she says."

Meanwhile, back on the message board, a prayer vigil of sorts was taking place, so everyone could give Penlind large doses of love and hope for her bouncing bundle of lies.

Then the email invitation arrived. I got a password and a link to a secret message board, where about a dozen people had gathered to do some fact-checking on our Penlind. They had been busy collecting all of her stories, copying and pasting them together, and combing through each claim. They were all women of varying ages and educational backgrounds who all doubted Penlind, and worried that the community was so smitten with her that they'd start sending her cash for medical care. It wasn't unprecedented; as a community we often sent out gifts to people who were expecting a baby, or a bit of cash to someone who had lost a job. The difference between those souls that were helped and Penlind, however, was that there were always a few people who had met them, and spent time with them offline. No one at The Bronze had ever even heard Penlind's voice on the phone.

The secret team of cynics called themselves the Bronze Investigation Team (or The BIT) to add humor to a sticky situation. Each woman assigned herself one of Penlind's claims to check for accuracy. Within a few days, the group discovered that the department at Harvard she claimed her husband chaired didn't exist, and that there was no archaeologist named "Riley" doing anything, anywhere. Querying doctors and nurses dredged up lots of information on her medical claims regarding "Djoser" and little of it made sense.

But our most damning evidence of Penlind's penchant for lying came from a call to a community college somewhere in Colorado. Penlind had left behind bits of truth in her stories, like dandruff flakes on a shiny mane of bullshit. One of the women of The BIT recognized her own college in a story Penlind told about being a professor. Another member of The BIT made some calls and, with no small amount of tenacity, found a student worker in the library who was a hydrant of information.

It was claiming to have a relative in The Barenaked Ladies that brought down Penlind, oddly enough. The band with the silly name set off a clanging bell in the student's head, and she told the story of a librarian who had made the very same claim. Her name was Penny. According to the student, Penny told lots of stories but had no children, and wasn't married. There was some sort of brouhaha about stolen computers that were found in her possession, and that was the last she saw of Penny.

I remember feeling that this woman had just gone too far. Some weird maternal instinct took over and I wanted to rip her fingers out at the roots so she'd be unable to spew those thick, noxious pleas for attention onto my beloved message board.

The BIT carefully made a list of the evidence, and prepared to go forth into the community to tar and feather the interloper.

*　　*　　*

This is where high school politics come into play once again. There are some laws related to internet discourse that rule over every forum, all over the Web. The most cited law is Godwin's Law, which states that

> As an online discussion grows longer, the probability of a comparison involving Nazis or Hitler approaches.

There is a tradition in many Usenet news-groups that once such a comparison is made, the thread is over and whoever mentioned the Nazis has automatically lost whatever argument was in progress.

It is considered poor form to arbitrarily raise such a comparison with the motive of ending the thread. There is a widely recognized codicil that any such deliberate invocation of Godwin's Law will be unsuccessful.

The second most cited law is likely Snacky's Law and that's the one that applied to The BIT and was an immense roadblock to getting the truth out to the masses. Snacky's Law says that

> Whenever two (or more) groups of people are arguing anywhere on the Web (Usenet, mailing lists, message boards, blogs, etc.), inevitably, someone on one side of the argument (regardless of age or gender) will compare the group on the other side to "those bitchy girls who made everyone's life hell in high school."

Every one of us in The BIT had been compared to those bitchy girls who made everyone's life hell in high school. At one time or another we had all, metaphorically, shoved some jackhole in a locker and soldered the combination lock permanently closed.

So many people believed so much in Penlind that any attempt by any one of us to discredit her would escalate into the invoking of Snacky's Law, and probably would end with the invoking of Godwin's Law as well. We would likely be compared to Nazis for sending bitchy girl vibes out into the world that would, surely, cause Djoser's death from negative dead baby/puppy vibes.

We needed to find someone beyond reproach. Someone whom everyone liked, respected, and who never got involved in kerfuffles. Someone who was a friend to everyone and who could carry the news out to our message board without incident. Every community has a person like this. At Whedonesque.com, his name is Simon. At Buffistas.org, her name is Nilly. At the The Bronze, her name was Margot. Margot was willing to calmly, soothingly carry the bag of evidence we had collected out into The Bronze. Our timing was a little off, since we chose to have Margot post the info dump on the day of a large cyber prayer vigil for Penlind's "son."

A dump truck full of shit hit the windmill.

That's the only way I can describe what followed Margot's post. Factions emerged between those who had been slightly suspicious of Penlind, those who had believed her completely but were reasonable when faced with the evidence of her lies, and those who staunchly defended the woman who had cruelly manipulated all of us for months. A fierce debate was launched, some accusing others of being heartless bastards, others accusing some of being willfully ignorant in light of the facts.

I was never angry at her defenders; I understood that no one wanted to believe that they lent their heart to a fraud. No one wants to be played for a fool—we all like to believe we're somehow smarter than that.

James Frey pulled the wool over Oprah's eyes with his memoir, *A Million Little Pieces,* and JT Leroy scammed half of Hollywood until *New York* magazine formed its own version of The BIT and pointed out that both of the emperors were buck naked, and one of them didn't even exist, really.

So there's no need to feel ashamed by being a little bit trusting, I think. I'd rather get burned once in awhile than lock myself away in a concrete drum of cynicism.

Penlind showed up briefly to make a dramatic exit from our community after chiding us for our heartlessness, which came pretty close to Snacky's Law, and she was never heard from again.

I read a story in *The Village Voice* once about a similar situation happening at a support forum for migraine sufferers. That community was so rocked by the betrayal of trust that it never recovered the sense of solidarity and solace that had once made it such an attractive place to seek support.

Our forum didn't fall apart, but then, we had suffered worse people than Penlind. We had fought off pedophiles, thieves, hackers, and stalkers to keep our community safe and strong and worth the considerable amount of time we all spent goofing off there.

I did receive a mysterious email about a week after we ran Penlind off the board, from an unfamiliar email address. The sender asked, "How did you find out that Penlind wasn't telling the truth?"

I squinted suspiciously at my screen and replied, "We were so much smarter than she was."

I just needed to make one last jab, just in case.

*   *   *

When I was doing some final fact-checking on this essay, I found an obituary for the woman who posted as "Penlind." She passed away a few weeks before I wrote this. I hope her troubled mind has found peace.

Party Politics

One cool night in West Hollywood, two warring factions, bathed in unflattering fluorescent light, made an unholy alliance. We were two sides of one fandom, locked in an ancient struggle of wit and will over a single moment in history: PBP Weekend.

They say that the road to hell is paved with good intentions. But actually? It's paved with crudités.

PBP stands for Posting Board Party—The Bronze posting board to be exact. It was an annual gala of epic proportions thrown by *Buffy* and *Angel* fans, for *Buffy* and *Angel* fans. The cast and crew of both shows would attend, along with four hundred or so fans from around the world. There was an auction to raise money for charity, an open bar in the VIP Lounge, very loud live music, and some sort of buffet buried in a back hallway somewhere. It was a gorgeous clusterfuck of a bash that everyone seemed to adore.

Everyone, that is, except about sixty or so of us Bronzers who thought that perhaps things had gotten way out of control with PBP. Sixty compared to four hundred likely seems a small, disgruntled, bitchy minority. And we were. The day-to-day reality of The Bronze was that we only had about a hundred and fifty or so folks stopping by the forum every week at a regular clip. Sure, there were hundreds of lurkers who read the boards religiously, but we were there providing the daily fodder.

PBP started out well enough. Generous handfuls of Bronzers showed up at a Hard Rock Café in West Hollywood and hobnobbed with producers and actors. It was way before my time, so I only heard anecdotes from those who were there, but it seemed like a good time. As the fandom grew, so did the party, and it became a distorted shadow of its once-intimate self. Old-school Bronzers would look around and wonder, "Who the fuck *are* these people?" No one knew. Word got out that there would be a huge bash where hot actors would dance drunkenly with fans, and suddenly, the yearly rush to buy tickets would crash a server in seconds. It became harder to move through the throngs of strangers crowding around random celebrities. It got harder to find the people you traveled thousands of miles to see.

Some started to complain. Loudly.

And so the war began. The PBP Committee was a handful of fans with a truckload of disposable income. They were savvy business folk: a JAG attorney, a CEO of a savings and loan, a trust fund baby, a guy who made a killing in real estate, and so on. I think there were nine, total, in the beginning. They were regulars at The Bronze who laid out the deposits, did all the planning, and honestly, worked their collective asses off to make the party happen every year in Los Angeles.

So when the complaints started, they got defensive, which, I think, was probably fair. The complainers were pissed that the people who charged themselves with representing the community were ignoring the pleas to stop expanding the party, to bring it back to its more intimate roots. This also seemed fair. If you're going to wrap yourself in the banner of the community and call your thing a Posting Board Party, it may be best to make sure that your constituents at the posting board are at least somewhat content with your party.

Things got uglier than three-day-old road kill. Accusations of financial evil deeds were lobbed over a line in the sand.

Finally, the head of PBP, Inc., a guy who chose the unfortunate moniker "Morbius the Vampire" as his screen name, threw down the gauntlet and said, "If you don't like the way we do things, throw your own party."

What a *fantastic* idea.

A tall redhead named Kristen picked up the gauntlet and hatched a plan. There would be a party the same weekend as PBP, in Los Angeles, for half the price. And thus, Caritas was born.

I had just moved to Los Angeles from Boston in October 2000. I was rather lonely and bored, and The Bronze mostly kept me from totally losing my shit while I searched for a job and a place to live. When Kristen threw her hat in the ring, I offered to help her out with any tasks that needed doing. I also became acutely aware that I had chosen a side. Suddenly, the PBP Committee was my enemy, and though I had never met any of these people, I *hated* them all.

Kristen threw a fabulous shindig at the Paramount Commissary. There were fifty or so attendees, a dessert bar with strawberries as big as my head, chocolate fondue, and the place was professionally decorated by Paramount as a gothic lounge. There were gargoyles and candelabra, and cocktail tables dressed in midnight blue linens. We all got drunk and danced until Paramount tossed us out at the end of the night. It would have been absolutely perfect if it hadn't come so close to breaking Kristen financially. Some kind souls over at *Buffy* and *Angel* had sent some signed scripts for auction to help Kristen pay for the party, so she just scraped by without losing her car to some sort of party repo man.

We proved that we could live without the PBP Committee. They proved they could live without us. Still, our community had split into factions, and we didn't really want to go on like that. It's exhausting to have to remember which side of an argument everyone is on, when there's a hundred or so people involved in the debate.

That's how we ended up at Mel's Diner one fall evening. Me, Kristen, Will from the PBP Committee, and Maya, a neutral party in the party wars. We had decided to make a compromise. On PBP weekend, Maya, Kristen, and I would throw a mixer on Friday night to welcome the Bronzers to L.A. It would be low-key, with space for dancing, and a quieter area for chatting with friends and munching on snacks. There'd be a DJ so we could control the noise level, and a raffle to add to the entertainment. No celebrities in attendance meant that the clusterfuck factor would be reduced to zero. And Bronzers could pay $20 at the door for it without having to spend the full $75 ticket price for attending PBP. At least everyone would be in the same room again.

The PBP committee would retain control of its usual Saturday bash. Maya and I would take over the charity auction, procure the items, and run the tables.

There was a suite set up in the hotel called Caritas, where the folks who enjoyed smaller gatherings could mingle and have the sort of party they liked.

*   *   *

The Bronze was at peace about PBP weekend for the first time in years. The Friday night pre-party was lavishly decorated with the headstones of dead characters, and Maya convinced a friend at a prop shop to lend us a full-size skeleton, candelabra, and assorted wrought iron goodies. We used Ouija boards and other divination games as centerpieces, along with boxes and boxes of Buffy chocolate bars. We even got a couple of members of the Caltech rugby team to play bouncers for the evening, which went over well with the mostly female crowd. Maya and I put together the most successful charity auction we'd ever had, complete with a stake autographed by Buffy herself, Sarah Michelle Gellar, that sold for $2,500. We were so fucking proud of that stake. It took two months, six faxes, and countless phone calls to get that little girl to sign the damn thing.

And Will turned out to be the dearest of dears, bailing me out of trouble from time to time. I'm so ashamed that I hated him so much back when I didn't even know his real name was Will.

Morbius the Vampire ended up being indicted on some sort of finance scandal. The newspaper report actually called him, "[Real Name] also known as Morbius the Vampire . . ." and then went on to describe some sort of thing about a building and something about tenants that I still don't understand.

But it did remind me that I'm so glad I always post as Allyson. So if I'm ever indicted for something, I won't be humiliated with a stupid alias in the newspaper report.

The Misery Effect

Sometimes a film or an episode of a television show hits a raw nerve with me: the plastic edges of the plasma screen sort of melt away, I feel completely absorbed by the story and the characters telling it, and, well, I think that's the point when entertainment becomes art. I stop thinking about the production values, and whether or not the actress on screen should maybe eat a cupcake or two. I completely suspend disbelief and become a voyeur in another world, a world so complete I can almost smell the freshly mowed lawn in a scene.

A great piece of filmmaking stays with me forever, affecting my view of the world, adding phrases and words to my vocabulary, infusing new colors into the way I express myself. If I ask someone to pass the salt and they reply, "As you wish," I know that's Westley's reply from *The Princess Bride,* and it rolls rainbow sprinkles on my plain vanilla request. The line, brought to life by actor Cary Elwes, spilled from the brain of writer William Goldman.

Consider this famous movie moment:

"You know you don't have to act with me, Steve. You don't have to say anything, and you don't have to do anything. Not a thing. Oh, maybe just whistle. You know how to whistle, don't you, Steve? You just put your lips together and blow."

Lauren Bacall smolders and flirts with Humphrey Bogart on screen in *To Have and Have Not.* But credit for the infamous line goes to the writers of the screenplay, Jules Furthman and William Faulkner.

Sure, the audience would probably prefer to curl up by a fire with the sexy Bacall, but for a dose of the flirty, dirty talk you'd need someone like Furthman or Faulkner playing a Cyrano-inspired game outside the bedroom window. The words that make us fall in love with a character most likely come from the mind of a pudgy, balding guy sitting at an Apple cinema display screen in his pajamas, eating cheese doodles, and chugging Red Bull by the case.

My heart belongs to the storytellers, the Willam Goldmans of the world who put pen to paper and spin the tales out on a page, creating something where moments before there was only a giant, white, terrifying void. Given the choice between the guy playing the Dread Pirate Roberts and the guy eating the bag of Cheetos at his typewriter, I'll always pick the guy with the orange fingers. However, we rarely see the guy with the orange fingers. *Buffy the Vampire Slayer* writer Jane Espenson once told me, "I think it's a given that, to fans, the characters are realer than the writers . . . they're not in our living room every week, like Buffy is."

Maybe that's why I feel so protective of writers, generally. It's easy to forget that they're the great and powerful Oz at work behind the curtain in a fabulous castle. That is, until the walls start crumbling and the toilet backs up in Emerald City. Then you start yanking the drapes back to find the asshole responsible for maintaining the fairy tale. It isn't until the story spirals down an unexpected. . . . no, an *unwanted,* path that some members of the audience want to seek out the person responsible for taking away their suspension of disbelief. Once the responsible party—the writer—is found, some fans try to impress upon the responsible party how much better the story was before the story took the unwanted path.

The 1990 film *Misery,* based on the book by Stephen King, was about a writer held captive and tortured by a fan who was angered beyond reason that he had "murdered" her favorite character in a series of romance novels. She hobbled the writer, kept him prisoner, and forced him to rewrite the story so that her favorite character would continue to "live."

That fan is alive and well and living on the internet. And she has friends. Many, many friends.

*   *   *

In my fandom, writers are revered, but usually not above the story, which is probably how it should be. Fans built websites in honor of the writers. There were fan clubs with cute names like "Jane's Junkies" and "Marti's Minions." Each site would have bios and all works credited to that writer. Those sites weren't so much a tribute to the individual, as to the individual's ability to spin a yarn.

Buffy creator Joss Whedon once told the fans on a message board, "Trust the tale, not the teller." I understand that, in a way. I just don't agree with it. What if you were on the Titanic and Edward John Smith told you to trust the ship, not the captain? When the ship goes down, you'll find me punching the captain in the neck, not setting fire to the starboard bow in retribution for its sinking.

It's not really an apt metaphor, of course. A story not going where my heart would like it to end isn't going to leave me floating in icy waters in the middle of the Atlantic

Ocean . . . but for some fans, you'd think their very lives hinge on whether the hero lives or dies.

Such was the situation that arose when a beloved character died one season on *Buffy the Vampire Slayer*. The character's name was Tara; Tara was in love with Willow, and they were lesbian witches. When Tara was shot to death in an episode called "Seeing Red," a small group of fans went apoplectic. Here's a sample posting, taking the writers to task for what she sees as an act of betrayal against the fans:

> I just don't know what to do. I'm breaking down in tears, four and five times a day, and I have no idea how I'm going to get through "Seeing Red" tonight. Even though my girl friend is coming over to hold my hand. Don't they know what they're doing to us?
>
> I just don't understand how they could hurt us this much.
>
> They PROMISED we could trust them. They promised.
>
> Not doing well at all. Assholes. They're just fucking assholes and I hate them all. I wish an earthquake would swallow every last one of them and bury them while they slowly starve to death.

After "Seeing Red," someone called forth a *Misery*-like jihad on the writing staff at *Buffy*. The writers couldn't drop by a message board and chat with fans without a drive-by Molotov cocktail of accusation being lobbed across cyberspace at their writerly heads by people who were angry about the episode.

In his essay, "It's Not Homophobia, But That Doesn't Make It Right: Creative Freedom, Responsibility and the Death of Tara," author Robert A. Black writes:

> No, the killing of Tara was not an act of homophobia, but that doesn't make it right. Through proper handling of the Willow/Tara storyline, Joss Whedon could have attained greatness as a pioneer and visionary in modern society, but instead he traded that in for the imagined self-importance of his own ego—and we have all been diminished because of it. (www.dykesvision.com/en/articles/homophobia.html)

Whenever someone uses "pioneer" as a noun, I think of that game, "Oregon Trail," and now I'm imagining Joss Whedon driving a wagon train full of lesbian witches to their homestead, the Sapphic Ranch, where lesbians never die of cholera, so we, the viewers, will never be diminished by the self-importance of his ego.

Sure, I rant and spew hyperbole all over the internet as well. I understand getting the pain out of your system. I have to draw the line at chasing down writers on message boards and showering them with acid hate bombs.

Tim Minear says that in a show like *Buffy*, there are no sacred cows, not even lesbian cows are sacred . . . and then he tells me that I shouldn't write that down. But I have to agree. I can't imagine following Annie Proulx around the internet and calling her an asshole because Jack died before Ennis came to his senses and they both lived happily ever after on a ranch in *Brokeback Mountain*. I just want to kiss her for breaking my heart so thoroughly. Maybe I'm just masochistic.

Jane Espenson, who was on the writing staff that broke the story of Tara's death, said, "When the fans got mad, they did so with the purest of motives—they felt that the show had given them a gift and then stomped on it. Of course they were angry. I just hope they see that our intention wasn't that. It was to create a tragedy that would evoke an emotional response. Which it did. We just didn't mean that the response would involve literal pain that extended beyond the hour of watching the show."

This is what makes me want to wrap my arms around the writer and shield him or her from fandom anger. This was a good episode of television. It was well-written, tragic, heartbreaking. I never really saw any arguments that the episode was poorly executed; it was just that some fans felt that the story belonged to the audience, that the writers had a responsibility to them that extended beyond the hour of the show.

Jane understood that the story they were telling bled into the hearts of viewers who held dear the tale of two women in love, and that seeing a gay couple being tender and romantic, funny and true on television was important to them. It was important partly because it was rare, partly because it was well-told, and mostly because it touched on something heterosexual folks take for granted: they were finally able to see a romance familiar to their real lives on national television every week. So that's no small thing. These fans drank deeply of the story, they could almost touch it, and maybe they felt a bit of ownership over it because it touched them so. Though the story touched the audience, the characters didn't actually belong to the audience. They belonged to the storytellers.

"I certainly know what it is to sit at home and find oneself disagreeing with a plot twist—those characters just wouldn't do that! The writers clearly don't understand their own characters! And you just know, deep in your soul, that the story just got wrong," says Jane, with no small amount of sympathy. "But, seen from the writers' point of view, we decide what actions the characters take and they don't have an existence outside of our decisions—if it feels right to us, then it *is* right, by definition."

Jane is so much cooler than I am. I felt hugely protective of the writers, angry on their behalf. Needlessly so, maybe. I write essays, and it seems so clear to me that the stories I tell are mine. You're welcome to read them, even buy them, but these are my words, my ideas that I've chosen to share. I'm free to keep these ideas to myself, or to share ideas you don't like. Joss Whedon was free to keep Tara to himself and never share, never allow anyone to enjoy that idea. He was free to smash that idea into the ground. Doesn't make him an asshole. He's just telling stories, and in the end, no one ended up choking on salt water in the middle of the Atlantic because Tara died.

I do, however, understand the sense of betrayal when a writer yanks the rug out from under the audience. I don't agree with it, rationally, but I get the visceral reaction. Tim Minear once said, "There will be an occasional happy, so that it can be crushed under the boot of the writer." Of course, his favorite movie is *It's a Wonderful Life,* so take that into consideration before thinking him completely sadistic.

So what's a fan to do when the story ends, besides going completely bugfuck on the internet? Do something productive and write your own stories, otherwise known as fan fiction, or fanfic, described by Jane as " . . . the wonderful stories created by fans that allow them to play in the same world we play in. I adore fanfic, and I think there are times when these stories can surpass the official product. Writing for the joy of creating exists in its purest form in fanfic."

I don't think Jane has ever read MPreg fic, in which two members of the boy band 'N SYNC get it on and then one miraculously gives birth to a gay lovechild. Still, I agree with her. In my head, Jack and Ennis do buy that ranch and sit by the fire at night, wrapped in each other's arms. It's not the truth of the story—that belongs to Proulx, the author. But it's a way for the story to go on in my head, a wish fulfilled in some small way. And Jane is right, some fanfic does surpass the official product. There are some fine writers out on the net, who have scooped up characters from series long-canceled and tucked them safely away onto their hard drives, to live forever. I swear, if you ever longed for an episode of *Miami Vice* where Crockett goes down on Tubbs, you can just Google your way to satisfaction. Seriously.

*   *   *

Most fans don't go nuts. They just enjoy the ride. Still others choose to voice their concerns using the good old-fashioned post office.

In the hallway outside the writers' offices at the television show *Angel,* there was a corkboard, littered with printed out emails from fans who became unhinged for one reason or another. *Angel* Producer Tim Minear recalls an email that began, "Dear Doyle Killer . . . " in reference to a lead character he killed off a few weeks earlier. Once, *Angel* Executive Producer David Greenwalt charged out of his office, stabbed a tack through a sheet of paper, and then returned to the office, slamming the door behind him. The email began, "Dear David Greenwalt (if that is your REAL NAME) . . ." As if someone who is paid for his skills of imagination couldn't come up with a better pseudonym than "Greenwalt."

There is a homeless guy in my neighborhood who stinks like he's been dipped in a vat of cat piss. He stands outside the grocery store on my corner yelling obscenities at the Coca-Cola machine. He lives right here in my neighborhood, has been hanging out by that Coke machine as long as I've been here; he is part of the community, for better or worse. That's sort of how I feel about crazy, obsessed *Misery*-ish fans.

They're still my people, and I don't wish them any specific harm. I just don't want to engage with them anymore than I want to stand downwind of the Coke Machine Taunter of Los Feliz, California.

The Corkboard of the Crazed outside the *Angel* offices certainly didn't represent fandom as a whole, but, as in any random sampling of society, there is a pocket of crazy people. I figure that the best I can do is to avoid standing downwind of the nutjobs and accept that as long as long as there are way fewer certifiable nutjobs than there are good neighbors, the fandom I'm in is still a pretty nice neighborhood.

Deus ex Machina

Think of a server as a large apartment building. The landlord of the building rents out units of space to tenants, who may live as they like within the parameters of the lease. You're free to walk around your unit naked as the day you were born. You're free to dance naked in front of the bathroom mirror to REO Speedwagon's "Keep on Loving You," or you could even smear ice cream on your ass while whistling a jaunty tune. As long as you don't put any big holes in the walls or stain the rug with bodily fluids from your weekly bloodletting rituals, the landlord is happy to take your rent money and leave you to your private freak show.

WILL THE VAMPIRE PEOPLE PLEASE LEAVE THE LOBBY?

You're also free to invite people over for beers and cheese dip and to have a spirited discussion on mercury levels in tuna fish. You can also leave your front door open so that people walking through the hallway can join the discussion. But if any of your guests inexplicably takes a crap on your kitchen floor and starts throwing feces at your friends, you're within your rights to toss the deranged party crasher.

Your website is just like your apartment. You rent space on a server, and you can use that space for a blog, an internet community, or to post pictures of your cat. Or for one of those god-awful wedding sites, where there will be a few pictures of unicorns playing under rainbows as the background to your Glamour Shot photo of you and your betrothed spooning happily against the fake background of an oak tree in autumn. This is the website equivalent of smearing ice cream on your ass while whistling a jaunty tune. Passerby may cringe at your freak show, and maybe complain to your landlord, but as long as you're not breaking any laws, the landlord will likely ignore the complaint or tell the complainant to stop looking in the window.

Such is the way of the net. Posting kiddie porn is breaking your lease and the law. For that you can be booted and arrested. Using your email to send thousands of advertisements for herbal Viagra is likely against your internet service provider's or your server owner's lease. Booted out on the street you will be, like a tenant who blasts Eminem at three in the morning to the chagrin of his or her neighbors.

It's likely understood by all that throwing someone out of your apartment or house because their behavior offends you or breaks the law isn't censorship. When you show someone the door, you are not Congress, and you are not making a law abridging the right to free speech. In the same way, a message board is only as democratic as the site owner/webmaster/moderator allows. A community moderator may be the tenant, landlord, super, or any combination of those things in an internet community. The moderator is the legislative, judicial, and executive branch of his or her own little community; it's a theocracy, and the site owner is the god in your machine, for as long as you're logged into a given site.

And yet, everyday on the net, some jackhole gets warned by a site owner or moderator to tone down obnoxious behavior. Undoubtedly, said jackhole will claim that his or her First Amendment rights are being violated on a public message board. To be clear, I'm all for freedom of speech. But in order for free speech to be enforced on the net, we'd need to hand the net over to the government and pay for it all with our tax dollars. And then we'd have all sorts of regulations to go with that free speech protection. We'd have government-owned servers run by Haliburton or that horse guy that ran FEMA. I don't want Congress deciding, regulating, or legislating anything about the net. I like the idea of the entire internet floating in international waters, where no treaty can touch it, on a pirate ship that never docks.

I love message board moderators the way some women love cops. There's something sexy about unbridled authority. Sure, "mods" don't have guns, but they can stomp the shit out of anyone in their jurisdiction. They're the sheriffs of their own dusty towns and can run anyone out with the flick of a finger across the home row.

*　*　*

In all my years as an internet drama social networking software enthusiast, I've drifted through all sorts of message boards in a series of one night stands and long-term relationships. They've all had different styles of moderation; from the community policing of Buffy.com's The Bronze to the jackbooted thugs at TelevisionWithoutPity.com (TWoP), I'm fascinated by the ways each board enforces the law of their particular slice of the internet.

TWoP is known for its iron-fisted style of hardcore moderation. It's important, because a site with dozens and dozens of forums about television shows is a Petri dish for the growth of obnoxious troll spores.

Glark, founder of TWoP, once broke up kerfuffles in his *West Wing* forum by forcing all the users to include quotes from *Star Trek: Wrath of Khan* in their posts or the posts would be deleted. It was a genius solution to prevent his board from spinning out of control into all-out flame wars due to arguing fan factions getting more irate with each other with each ill-advised post. He's also used quotes from Ralph Wiggum of *The Simpsons*. The silliness of it cuts the stress and also forces the user to think before posting. Forcing the users to look up quotes to use with their posts gave the users a minute to think before hitting the "Send" button. Genius. TWoP mods will also close a forum down for a time-out if a forum gets too hairy. Sometimes they'll burn a forum down, salt the earth, and have a keg party on its decaying corpse. At least, my secret fantasy is that they do that. They might just delete the forum and forget it ever existed the next day. But I hope they at least have a beer after pulling the plug.

Whedonesque.com is equally iron-fisted in its moderation approach, with a moderator in just about every time zone in order to keep a watchful eye on a site that can turn on a dime from friendly to fandom explosions of drama. They also shut down registrations to the site to keep the user numbers at a manageable level.

Why the need for all this moderation? Why are there captains poking swords at scalawags, prodding them down a plank toward the open sea? Mutiny, of course. Trolls of all sorts gather in the bowels of the ship, hitching a ride and puking up their plague-ridden posts all over message boards. Trolls are awful gremlin-minded people whose main purpose is to throw an internet community into chaos. They're the younger sibling disrupting the slumber party with catcalls and insults outside the bedroom door. They can be a minor irritant, and they can actually offer some levity to a discussion board soaking in pomposity. Most trolls, however, fall into an abusive category of torment, vandalism, and perpetual harassment until they're pushed overboard by a moderator. Even then, the sticky bastards may return as a "sockpuppet," the name for when the same sticky bastard registers with a new user name, pretends to play nice for five minutes, and then instantly morphs into the same old cackling lunatic. If the moderator keeps deleting the troll's accounts and the community doesn't respond at all, the troll disappears. They're like the monster under your bed; if you stop believing in it, it will cease to exist.

Troll tactics for community disruption are often ridiculous, but people like me can't resist the bait. I am, to the troll, like a fish in a barrel. For example

Troll: As the great-great grandson of Walt Whitman, I feel that no one understands *Leaves of Grass* the way I do.

Forum resident: Walt Whitman didn't have children. He didn't fuck women, he was like, proud and out and dancing on the civil war gay pride wagon float.

Troll: Are you calling me a liar?

Forum resident: Yes. Yes I am.

Troll: I'm getting my internet lawyer to sue you for slander.

Moderator comes in and tells everyone to chill the fuck out.

Troll: Freedom of speech! Buncha fascists! Hitler!

Moderator presses eject button.

Troll's Sockpuppet, Jim: Hi. I'm new. I think you people are all awesome, but you were really harsh on Troll. I mean, do any of you have proof that Walt Whitman didn't have kids?

Rinse, repeat. This is, of course, the abridged version of a flame war, where participants in a community verbally kick the crap out of each other. This is when the gods in the machine come in handy, swooping in all swashbuckly to clean house. I'm pretty libertarian about the internet. I want as few rules as possible, but in order for that to work, everyone sailing through needs to have a sense of fair play or we'd just end up with an ocean full of ghost ships ramming into each other haphazardly. The entire point of trolling is schadenfreude—the mirthful glee at witnessing others in frustration, anger, pain. There's a bit of sadism to it, as well. I mean, I like watching stupid people claw at their own brains in frustration just as much as the next person, but a troll is more of a cow-tipper. It's not clever, it's just lame. If I'm just standing there, chewing cud, minding my own business, why you gotta come by and shove me in the mud, troll?

*   *   *

Message boards without active moderators allow the user, or the community as a whole, to shove back. The Bronze was a privately owned website. The server space was leased out to The WB network by a company called Apollo Interactive. Apollo was an absentee machine god. The Bronze was a "self-policing" (read: helpless) community. There'd often be long battles between two or more groups of people over how to deal with jerks who couldn't manage to type a coherent sentence, hurled insults at other users, screwed with the programming codes, or otherwise shat on the kitchen floor.

But even though there's no sheriff in town, the trolls have to be dealt with. The choices in a self-policing community, which has no access to programming tools needed to ban an offensive user, are as follows:

Do Not Feed the Energy Creature (DNFTEC): This tactic is based on the concept that if you ignore bad behavior, it will wither away and die like an unwatered Ficus. This is based on the idea that assholes, or trolls, on the internet survive on the attention of the annoyed. They suck the energy from a community and move on, like a cyber locust. In the olden days before the internet, you'd take this sort of person for a ride out into the woods and shoot them, as Darwin intended, before he could spawn. On the net you can shun, which was the nonviolent olden days way to punish someone. By ignoring the undesirable asshole, he or she eventually starves and dies out in the cold, or moves on to another community.

Give the Troll the Hugs Daddy Never Gave: People who employ this concept are the worst. The idea is that the asshole wreaking havoc on the community is only misbehaving because he or she is some sort of wild child who has been raised by wolves with high-speed internet access. If only we all cuddled the asshole and sang Kumbayah, the asshole would become fully integrated into society, get a job, pay taxes, and bring Toll House cookies to the block party. Troll Huggers think it'll work out like the way Mel Gibson befriended that kid with the boom-a-rang and the heavy metal hairdo in *Mad Max*. It never actually does work, and the wild child just keeps biting at the neighbors and then hiding under the aprons of the Kumbayah crowd, who insist that the wild child wouldn't bite if everyone else would just remember to walk on eggshells.

Cut a Bitch: This is how I deal with assholes on the internet. It's a quick, ruthless, cheap shot of a response to trollish behavior. It's a wicked post meant to make someone cry or have a complete meltdown. This is also known as flaming. It almost never works. Once at Buffistas, I asked a woman named Zoë if she perhaps had a brain injury of some sort, because she was behaving oddly, and I was very concerned. Perhaps she should consult a doctor? I couched all my meanness in terms of concern for the woman's health while telling her that she was exhibiting all the signs of a severe head injury, that she couldn't make a rational argument, was hysterically paranoid, and seemed unaware that she was a social outcast. As it turned out, she did have a brain injury, or at least claimed she did, and added that I was making her very depressed. The community at large spanked me for my transparent attempt to tell Zoë that she was a moron. But she was eventually banished from the board, anyway, so I felt like a winner.

Cut a Bitch most often results in Feeding the Energy Creature and causing a message board to boil out of control. Some community members will dramatically flounce off the board in frustration, hoping other members will beg them to stay. It's as sure as $E=MC^2$, actually. The flouncer will then return within the hour, with some lame excuse about not letting other people spoil his or her fun. It's a bizarre little dance around the troll, like a cyber maypole, with hyperbole.

I always go with Cut a Bitch because I'm a jerk, and I walk a fine line between Troll and Valued Community Member. I get to be an asshole with just cause. But I always sincerely apologize for it afterward. I vaguely remember tracking down a thirteen-year-old troll's father once, and emailing him a list of reasons why the internet was not his son's baby-sitter, and now the internet knows where his son lives. He never responded, and the thirteen-year-old showed up a couple of weeks later in a rage about being grounded and that I HAD NO RIGHT to tattle on him. Meh. It just felt *sooo goood*. I should note that I was twenty-eight at the time. Tattling on a thirteen-year-old. We're all pathetic in our own special ways.

*   *   *

I'm deeply ashamed to admit relishing in my own mean-spiritedness at times. I found there was something cathartic about the Cut a Bitch method. I didn't fully appreciate that until there was no reason to use it, and I found that it was frustrating to not be able to express my rage at stupidity. For the ultimate in troll-free environments, there's The Well. I joined The Well a couple of years ago when I was tired of arguing about the best way to deal with trolls over at Buffistas.org. I decided to take a sabbatical from the growing pains of the co-op board, and to try out an explosion-free environment.

The Well, housed at Salon.com, is one of the oldest message boards, and just celebrated its twentieth anniversary. The Well isn't just moderated; it's pay-to-play. Fifteen dollars a month is the subscription price. Everyone at The Well posts under their own names, so there is no anonymity. When I signed up at The Well, a moderator called me to make sure I was an actual person, welcomed me to the community, and answered my questions about rules and social norms. It's a clever way to weed out trolls who would otherwise wreak havoc on the stoic discussion boards. It's harder to make a jackass out of yourself without the cloak of anonymity, in front of people who have your credit card information, and after you have signed terms of service agreement.

I was a disappointed member of The Well. They had advertised "spirited discussions" but there was no intensity to the conversations. I navigated over to the television forums and found people just sort of posting random thoughts without any sort of passion. I couldn't find a foothold anywhere. It was as if the spirit of the boards had been sandblasted away by time.

I realized that it reminded me of the time I went to my friend Jacqui's wedding in Iowa. I was outside having a smoke late at night, and heard this awful hum. I asked Jacqui if she could hear it. "Yes . . . it's crickets!" she told me, incredulously.

Well, it's not that I hadn't heard crickets; it's that I'd never heard crickets unaccompanied by the ambient noises of a city. That's sort of what The Well was like. I was a scrappy city mouse experiencing culture shock.

Sometimes the sound of sirens off in the distance is just a reminder that the world hasn't ended. There are other people around and annoying as they may be, as long as I can hear them living their lives, I'm comforted to know that zombies haven't taken over the Earth. At The Well, I kept picturing everyone sitting around a fireplace in an oak library, smoking pipes, sipping cognac, and wearing dinner jackets. I missed the motley group of pirates outside the safety of The Well's fortress of crickets. So I canceled my subscription and headed back out into the uncharted waters of low moderation, where I can let my inner troll loose when it needs a bit of exercise. You might want to keep your thirteen-year-old sons off of my lawn.

The Bronze Is Dead.
Long Live the Bronze!

There have been two online forums in my life that have held my attention long enough to settle in and make the sort of friends I'd venture out of my comfy apartment to meet off line. I'm really determined to become agoraphobic, so it's a huge deal for me to actually put on shoes and find my keys to go break bread with someone whose face I've never seen.

My current main squeeze is Buffistas.org, which has surprisingly little to do with its roots in the *Buffy* fandom anymore. It's mostly a place to discuss the many uses of salad shooters and bitch about work.

But my first forum love, The Bronze, died a nasty death

at the hands of ridiculously stupid television network executives on July 10, 2001.

The Bronze was located at Buffy.com and named after the nightclub on *Buffy the Vampire Slayer*. Now when you type in the URL, you get a terrible 404 File Not Found error. Websites don't get grave markers. They really should, given how melodramatic we Bronzers could be.

It all started with a bidding war. The WB network was negotiating with 20th Century Fox to lease another two years of *Buffy*. The WB had been home to *Buffy* for five years and had been hosting our web community for all that time. That means they were footing the bill for our message board; we fans were living on the WB's dole. We watched the negotiations unfold with great interest, since our cyber playground was at stake. We didn't want to get lost in the network kerfuffle and wake up to find the message board gone, with no recourse. Things weren't going well, Fox wanted oodles more money, the WB didn't want to pay much more, and then a struggling little network called UPN threw its hat in the ring. UPN, desperate to acquire the critical darling and the four to five million weekly viewers, won the bidding war.

So our Slayer girl was changing networks. We got the news in May 2001. We all started packing. Did I say *packing?*

I meant *panicking*. We had no idea what would become of the forum. And no one would tell us.

A lot of us felt a sense of ownership over the forums. We had no moderators, no one who could ban troublemakers, and no one to fix technical glitches. When the board first opened, the designer, James Lamb (who met his wife on The Bronze message board) would help out with such things, and then when management changed, we had a nice fellow named Justin Woo to do the job. But after a couple of years, the moderator faded into oblivion and the community became self-policing; our only options were to collectively shun undesirable people, or if we had a particularly nasty forum troll, to do a WHOIS search on the user's IP address and report a terms of service violation to the troll's service provider. If none of that makes sense, allow me to translate: We emailed AOL and told them to report the jackass to mommy and daddy, who would then ground the forum troll, or so we hoped.

Having no contact with our silent benefactors meant we weren't getting any information about whether The Bronze would shut down for good, or if UPN would just take over paying for the board's bandwidth.

We had a small backup forum set up on my friend Kristen's server, called The Refugee Camp, which we used to meet up when we had board outages, but there was no real way she could host the entire community indefinitely. It would have been a financial nightmare.

So we waited for news and continued chatting throughout the summer, ignoring the rather large meteor in the sky careening toward our home. Denial is awesome. But then, one day in July, about two months before Buffy would premiere on its new network, we received word from the company hosting The Bronze: The WB yanked the contract, and The Bronze would be closing in the next twenty-four hours.

You know those Japanese *Godzilla* movies where the whole city of Tokyo screams and runs in zigzag directions under the shadow of the terrible lizard? The last twenty-four hours of The Bronze were the cyber equivalent of that. The text color for fans posting messages was beige on a black background. Other colors were reserved for VIPs: the actors, writers, and other production folk involved in making the show. It was easier to find their messages against the black if one was quickly scrolling for information. During the last few hours, etiquette be damned, everyone chose a different colored text, so it looked less like an orderly message board and more like a mess of fireworks. There was a certain franticness to it all, racing to get every thought entered before the plug was pulled and the code that held the place together was shelved.

A gaggle of *Buffy* writers all came to the board to post eulogies to the forum. Bronzers who had left their fandom days behind years before returned to post into the big black board one last time before it was taken off line.

Somewhere in the back of my head, I was convinced that it would only be a few days and we'd all be posting on the same space again, maybe on a different server, but all would be well.

But that was really the end. The Bronze was taken off line and the code that made it what it was ended up in a jar on a dusty shelf, forgotten behind a can of cream of mushroom soup. I just didn't know that at the time, and so I jumped on my horse and put on my riding hat, prepared to tilt at windmills with all the fury I could muster.

A few kind souls set up internet refugee camps where we Bronzers hunkered down until our glorious forum returned on UPN's servers. We watched and waited.

A few weeks before *Buffy* was to begin its sixth season on the new network, The Bronze reopened for forum business. So we stormed ashore and rammed our flag deep into this new forum, claiming it for Bronzer Nation. And as we looked around the new digs, we realized something . . . it sucked. It wasn't *our* Bronze; it was *a* Bronze. The format of the board was unwieldy. It was difficult to read and post. It didn't archive properly. It required registration, so we had to rush and claim our screen names. It smelled funny, like cheese, feet, cigars, and butt juice. We hated it. We demanded satisfaction. After all, we were paying . . . well, we weren't paying anything for it. This may have been our biggest problem. Beggars, of course, can't be choosers. That wasn't about to stop me from making demands, though.

The company charged with the design of the new Bronze website was called NextLeft. Its slogan was "We provide solutions that work." If it doesn't work, it's not a solution, right? Right. They were the enemy. My friend Maya and I started making calls to UPN and NextLeft, pleading for them to purchase the old code from the previous site host and then leave us alone. Our online community had scattered to different forums all over the web. The diaspora was distressing. NextLeft couldn't seem to provide a solution that worked for us.

With our community swirling around the bowl, and no signs of change occurring on the message board, we decided that we had to take action. Someone suggested letting a herd of goats loose in UPN's lobby, or perhaps hiring those jackasses from the anti-smoking "Truth" campaign to dress up like the Donner Party and eat each other outside NextLeft's office (two birds, one stone). In the end, we chose the grassroots letter-writing campaign as a polite means of telling the network that its website sucked. In hindsight, we should have gone with the "Truth" people.

Assuming that a little star power would help us appear scary and powerful to the network, we got online and contacted a friend who knew Amber Benson, a regular on *Buffy*. Within a half hour, Amber posted her support of our campaign to get The Bronze back online. The next morning, I called *Buffy* creator Joss Whedon's office to let him know what we were up to. I did it both as a courtesy, and with the hope that Whedon would make a call to UPN, and suddenly, everything would be okay again. Since we had energy to burn, we continued to campaign while waiting to hear back from Camp Whedon.

Driven by internet word-of-mouth, the postcard campaign got into full swing. We were invited to appear on a weekly college radio/internet broadcast to discuss our efforts. Because I am secretly twelve years old, I decided to call both UPN and NextLeft for comment, before appearing on a "National Radio Broadcast." A very annoyed man named Mo was apparently assigned to take our calls at NextLeft. It was obvious from Mo's tone that he had a great deal of hatred in his heart toward us, the site, and the show. He had no comment other than that they would work on the site " . . . if and when UPN pays NextLeft to do so." Mo blamed The WB for not cooperating when asked for information about the message board. It was beyond Mo's understanding that the network that lost the bid for *Buffy* may have been reluctant to aid the network that won the bid in its internet marketing campaign.

Armed with Mo's Lame Excuse, I called UPN for comment. Once Maya and I identified ourselves as the people behind the postcard campaign, the marketing director was anxious to speak with us. We snitched on Mo the Annoyed Guy, and were informed that UPN was calling an emergency meeting with NextLeft to discuss our concerns. Then we drove up to Long Beach to be interviewed, and since we were so young and foolish, we told everyone that we thought there would be a resolution soon.

That week, Scifi.com put a report on the wire about the campaign to revive our message board, which further bolstered our confidence. It was soon after that that we received word from UPN that our pal Mo was no longer employed by NextLeft. We probably should have felt bad, but as we saw it, NextLeft was killing our community, and it only seemed fair that they should receive a casualty or two as well. We mistakenly took this as a sign that the network was taking us seriously.

Eventually, UPN assigned a friendly young man named Matthew to help out with the web marketing for Buffy.

Matthew proved to be our only advocate in the matter of The Fans vs. The Inept Network. Matthew proposed that we should meet and discuss the problem, and invited a guy named Clayton from NextLeft, who, one would suppose, would find a solution that worked.

I suggested meeting for dinner at the Saddle Ranch. It's a chop house in West Hollywood, with a mechanical bull and obscenely hot waitresses. It's a sort of raucous place filled with people wanting to be seen by other people who want to be seen by infinity. I've no idea why I thought this was a good meeting location other than the fact that I thought if I stumbled over my own tongue, maybe they wouldn't hear me. I was armed with a folder full of demographic information, a list of published articles on internet communities citing The Bronze, and a financial report of the money Bronzers spent advertising the show through charity parties and ads in industry trade magazines. I was dressed in a navy suit, trying to look like anything but the stereotypical internet junkie with a worn out t-shirt with airbrushed dragons on the front and elastic-waist high-water jeans. It was a pitch meeting, basically. I had to convince them to fund our twenty-four hour bullshit sessions.

Matthew told me to be patient. He would figure it all out. He probably thought I was insane and was just trying to avoid getting a fork in the eye while I sang "Oh Danny Boy" while bathing in his blood. I never got a chance to tell Matthew that I liked him and appreciated his bravery in meeting me, the head cheerleader of crazy internet fandom. There was some sort of restructuring at UPN and Matthew, along with dozens of other useful people, found himself unemployed, and we Bronzers lost our only advocate with the power to help us.

Unless, of course, our hero, Joss Whedon, creator of our television universe, would finally hear our cries of agony and do right by us, the fans.

Eventually, our god spoke. However, god forgot his password, so it was hard to recognize him.

I may have trouble convincing you I'm Joss says:
(Wed Oct 17 02:45:00)

Hello. i may have trouble convincing you i'm joss, but I really am. I mean, even more than usual. I'm SO Joss that . . . it doesn't matter. Only the information I have is important. And I don't actually have any. EXCEPT THIS: I have spoken to the brass a UPN very specifically about getting a real posting board on the site. They're

new at this, but it's gonna happen. And we will
chat and there will be colors and all will be well.
Just be patient.

And patient I was. The Bronze, it would seem, was hidden
somewhere in Godot's back pocket. We never did get it back.
There's a site called BronzeBeta.com that resembles the old
layout, and a lot of us Bronzers posted there until *Buffy*'s
series finale on May 20, 2003. It was never really the same,
despite the best intentions of the fans who tried to resurrect
the spirit of our beloved Bronze.

I wish we had the foresight of my precious Buffistas.org
denizens. When the Buffistas learned that they would be losing their free ride at Salon.com, they packed everything up,
collected tons of money, and designed a similar forum. It took
about a year to iron out the politics of the move, but now the
Buffistas are community-owned and moderated. We're not at
the mercy/charity of any corporation or network, which is
how it should be, really. It was a solution that worked.

The Internet Wants Your Daughters

Sometimes while I'm getting ready for work in the morning, I turn on the television for some background noise and time checks. At 7:25, the local news and weather broadcast comes on, and I know it's time to get in the shower. At 7:55, the same news and weather report comes on and I know I need to haul ass if I'm going to have enough time to grab a double vanilla tea latte from the Coffee Bean before work.

In between these time checks, *Good Morning America* chatters mindlessly about Iraq, Emeril's peach cobbler, and shamelessly pimps whatever movie its parent company, Disney, is premiering the following weekend. It's rare that I'll stop and actually look at the television screen in the morning, until they introduced a weeklong series on The Dangers of the Internet. Cue foreboding music. I put down the eyeliner mid-application and sat down on the couch in rapt attention.

The lesson Charlie, Diane, and Robin taught me is that the internet runs solely on the blood of virgin teenage girls. Oh yes, parents: The Internet Wants Your Daughters. Every blue-eyed girl with extra shiny hair who has ever gone missing will not be found in a shallow grave or weirdo comet-worshipping cult. They likely have been swallowed whole by MySpace.com in order to make the site load faster. Their sacrifice is to the gain of a million unhappy teenagers who quote Nine Inch Nails lyrics on their web pages to let the world know that the depth of their souls is a bottomless pit of angst. (Kids today are fortunate to have Trent Reznor to describe the winter of their discontent. I had Simon LeBon, and "Rio" never really helped me express my dark rage at the world.)

The *Good Morning America* series featured one story after another of young women duped into some sort of dangerous situation through the use of social networking software on the net. It's the cyber version of taking candy from strangers. The gist of it is that the computer creates a barrier that provides a sense of safety for people to express themselves, free of consequence. There you are, sitting in your favorite chair, behind a locked door, in your comfort zone. You're free to bleed to anyone who will listen to your secret hopes and fears. It's easy to forget that everything you're posting is on display in a window that anyone with a computer and a modem can read. It's not a private confessional with just your priest on the other side of the darkened slats; we're all fish in a bowl, unaware of the world outside staring at us . . . unless someone walks up and taps on the glass.

Charlie, Diane, and Robin were focusing primarily on a social networking website called MySpace.com. The site was originally intended for musicians to be able to share their music with each other, and get a bit of exposure. Each user can get an account for free, post photographs, upload music, keep a diary, and receive messages from the hundreds of "friends" that they add to their network. It's truly a fantastic bit of software when you think about how many people can connect with each other.

My first experience with MySpace, way back before it completely devolved into the suburban mall of the internet, was creepy and weird. I had a little profile and journal, and found that I was attracting middle-aged men with pockmarked leather faces and bleached mullets at an alarming rate. They all wanted to be my friend, and all were working "in the industry." So I pulled the plug on my profile and decided that weighing myself while wearing a wet snowsuit would improve my self-esteem faster than befriending guys who found Christ on a prison furlough. My second experience with MySpace was bandwidth theft through hotlinking. MySpace users tend to link directly to any image they want on the web and use that image on their personal page. Without getting into the boring technical explanation, it just means that users are then piggybacking on unsuspecting website owners. When someone "hotlinks" from one of my web pages, they're sucking my bandwidth. It's sort of like if a person started stealing minutes from your cell phone plan so you had to pay an overage charge every month for someone else's bullshit conversations.

It's possible that I am biased against MySpace for the reasons stated, and I acknowledge that there are many fine people who enjoy the site and the connections to others they have made by using it.

Back to you, Charlie, Diane, and Robin.

But still, the shrill warnings about the internet border on hysteria to my ears. MySpace has become the window to little Polly Klaas' bedroom, where some scumbag is about to crawl in to rape and murder our little girls. The answer for many parents is to nail the window shut, arrange for play dates, and don't let the kids play on the front lawn. Pick them up from school in a tank-like Hummer as if the path home is through downtown Iraq instead of the suburbs. Perhaps the internet is cruising slowly down suburban streets at dusk, lurking, stalking, waiting for the one freckled child whose parents are crazy enough to let play hopscotch on the drive-way, to then POUNCE!

I remember taking the bus into the city when I was twelve to go to the mall with friends. I shared a paper route for an evening edition paper that would have me knocking on stranger's doors after dark to collect money. I'm still alive, twenty years later. I don't believe that city kids are made of tougher material, but maybe city parents are. My mom was a big believer in "if someone hits you, hit them back twice as hard." There's power in that concept beyond the simple direction. No one has the right to hurt me, scare me, or make me do anything I know is wrong. So if some middle-aged man in a tan sedan rolled up next to me and whispered, "Hey, c'mere for a minute," I felt empowered to screech, "Fuck you, asshole!" and bolt. I'd strongly suggest this approach to parents. Give your kid permission to screech obscenities first and then run. It's far more satisfying to be able to punch the guy in the face, even if it's just verbally, than to feel like a slow-running gazelle on the plains. Plus, as an added bonus, your kid will have just called attention to the creepy car guy.

The same rules apply to some strange dude pulling up to your daughter's screen name on the internet. And that's sort of how it needs to be presented. The immediate danger isn't apparent when one is wrapped in the safety of one's own home, but I think parents need to be clear that giving out personal information to strangers on the internet presents the same risk.

I've run across my fair share of creepy jackholes on the internet, but I was an adult when I became involved in online communities, with a fully developed sense of judgment. The online communities I frequented weren't isolated, like a personal MySpace page, so there were lots of people participating in the conversations. Because I was mostly posting on easily accessible websites with fellow *Buffy the Vampire Slayer* fans, I often saw posts by teenage girls and boys who were participating in conversations with adults—strangers. Luckily, our message board was filled with women, a lot of them moms, attorneys, PhD students . . . all sorts of women keeping an eye out for each other, and for the kids who would post at our board. It didn't happen often, but it did happen on occasion that we would have problems with adult men who had a fondness for young, troubled girls, who would email and instant message the girls off-board, where the watchful eyes of hundreds of adults couldn't intervene. This sort of behavior would result in all-out message board wars, with the attendant threats of libel-slander defamation suits, arguments about the age of consent in New Zealand, and if consent can actually be given by a fifteen-year-old girl with a history of self-mutilation.

It sounds eye-rollingly melodramatic, I know. But it was happening in our internet community, and there's no way we could let that shit slide. We wanted our boards to be a safe playground for fans of any age. Most of us were and are aware of the stereotype of the internet junkie as the axe-murdering, pedophiliac predator. I think it was just as important to us in preserving our own identities as good, normal folks as it was a moral obligation to protect our younger community members from harm.

With all this talk about predators slinking around MySpace with yellow glowing eyes and razor-sharp teeth, there's also a lot of talk about what MySpace's responsibility is to protect the virtue of our girls from every Humbert Humbert with a web cam. I don't know what the answer is. It's way more complex than innocent, virginal blonde girls being stalked and exploited. Let's just be super-honest about everything and lay the hard truth out on the page: Some of our innocent, cherubic little darlings are exploring their sexuality out there on the net. And that is a natural, normal exploration. It includes taking part in dirty conversations, posting risqué photos of themselves, and looking at pictures of other people's naked bodies, or of other people having sex. All normal, all part of the natural curiosity that comes with puberty.

There are all sorts of weird questions we have about our bodies when we're stumbling through thirteen. Most of them all focus on one question: Am I normal? It's a hard question to ask mom and dad. It's a hard thing to discuss with your sons and daughters. Peers are for shit in this regard because they're just as clueless and paranoid. All I learned in sex ed is that I have fallopian tubes. Information used to be much harder to find, but that never stopped any of us from exploring our own sexuality and sometimes learning about it from a sixteen-year-old boy who learned about sex by jerking off to pictures in daddy's collection of *Penthouse* magazines. Now one can simply do a Google search to learn about blowjobs and the many kinds of waxing available. All of that natural, normal curiosity can be sated with a search engine, or a conversation with a pervert who digs how your daughter looks in her field hockey uniform.

Having said all this about what is normal and natural, it's important to point out that while bowel movements are normal and natural, one shouldn't crap his or her pants on a city bus in rush hour. We teach our kids that this is socially unacceptable when they're three years old, and they learn to go in a potty, as is right and proper. We teach our kids to look both ways before crossing the street so they won't get squashed by a car, and to not put a fork in the electrical outlet. If you're alive, if your kid is alive, they learned those safety lessons well. You don't expect electricity to take responsibility for your kids' health. Why expect the internet to prevent your kid from getting hurt?

A teenage kid playing peek-a-boo with a grown man on the internet is voluntarily walking into traffic, blindfolded. A teenage kid posting pictures of herself in nothing but a pair of panties and a smile is taking a crap on the express bus. It's unacceptable. If kids can learn to control bowel movements at the age of three, they can learn safer ways to get answers about sex and sexuality than via MySpace. You taught them how to use a potty, and how to avoid getting rundown by an SUV, you can most certainly call your local Planned Parenthood and set up an appointment with a counselor to help coach you through The Talk. You can always put a copy of *Our Bodies, Ourselves* on your daughter's desk. At least the information therein is medically sound, and answers all sorts of questions about what is normal.

Charlie, Diane, and Robin discussed none of this on *Good Morning America.* They did, however, talk some sense about computer safety, such as putting the family computer in the living room, or other high traffic area, where it's impossible for some piece of shit to send your kid web cam images of his penis without your noticing. Get yourself a MySpace account so that you can monitor your kids' profiles. Take an interest in their online friends. And, while you're doing all of that, it would be super awesome if you corrected their spelling. Chatspeak is nauseating, lol lol.

The web is just a random sampling of the first world societies who created it. Little league coaches, priests, teachers, and counselors have all been locked up for hurting kids. The response to that is to empower your kids to be tough, strong, and vigilant, not to lock them up in a bomb shelter until you release their pale, socially retarded shells out into the world at the age of eighteen.

Using the internet to connect with one's peers around the world is a truly amazing technological gift. It shouldn't be treated like a dark van with a greasy driver waving lollipops at kids walking home from school. To do so shortchanges kids of the miracle of social networking, of blogs and research, of information sharing and the free exchange of ideas with people half a world away. It's a new, scary thing that has created extraordinary changes in how we relate to each other and the world around us. Like the car was, like birth control was, like the telephone was, like air travel was. And when each of those things started seeping into the mainstream, Chicken Little proclaimed the sky was falling and that the downfall of society was nigh. So here we are again, with some hunkered in the basement, wearing helmets, when the answer is usually as simple as installing a safety belt and enjoying the ride.

Save Firefly

The cockpit smells like fireworks and sawdust; the smell an echo of the explosions that occurred an hour earlier. The control panel appears to have been lifted from a trashcan by an angry raccoon searching for sustenance. It's scratched, dented, and crusty in spots. Sitting in the pilot's seat, my feet don't touch the floor and I have to lean forward to reach the steering wheel. I feel like Lily Tomlin's Edith Ann being swallowed by that really big rocking chair.

A cute boy in a Civil War-ish soldier's uniform winks at me and tells me it's a go for launch, while my friend Kristen raises an eyebrow and grins. I imagine them steadying themselves as I grab the wheel. I'm the Sally Ride of this particular spaceship, which is anchored to a soundstage on Pico Boulevard at 20th Century Fox Studios. I'm on the set of *Firefly*, a television program that has just been canceled. This is the final week of shooting.

Firefly was a sci-fi show in danger of cancellation before the first episode ever aired. It was created by Joss Whedon, TV writer extraordinaire. My friend Kristen and I read the script for the pilot episode of *Firefly* months before it was broadcast. It sucked. It had no bite, no edge, no buzzwords meaning "devastatingly hip." Having been delirious fangurls of Whedon's previous creations, at first we were disappointed by our hero, but then settled into sort of reveling in a juicy mirth similar to that of every non-New Yorker's glee when the Yankees lose a big game. We loved Whedon when he was the underdog auteur, but now he was a big-time producer with no time to chat and play with us little fans anymore. We were bitter.

If you asked us then if we'd end up spending the holidays feverishly mounting a campaign to save this show from its inevitable cancellation, we would've laughed. But what we hadn't counted on was a guilt-inducing birthday gift, a plea for help from a worried wife, and our own abilities to lead an army of fangeeks into battle.

Our journey began when a small plea was posted to the internet by a fellow fangurl named Kiba to sign a petition in support of *Firefly*. Kiba had received a link to the petition from Whedon's wife Kai who was worried that her husband's latest labor of love was spiraling down the bowl, unable to grab a large enough audience to make the show profitable.

I dropped Kiba an email, explaining that online petitions were for losers. No one cared about them, and who would see it, anyway? No one reads internet petitions. You can sign with as many email addresses as you have, and most people have several: the one you use for work, the one you use for friends, the one where all your spam goes, the one you use for porn. Four hundred signatures on an internet petition equals two-hundred and thirty-seven people with too much time on their hands.

You'd have to deliver the petition to someone at the network who had decision-making power, genuinely liked the show, and was in a position to advocate for it. Judging from the advertisements Fox put together for *Firefly,* the network not only didn't understand their product, they were determined to have it bite the curb and stomp on its head.

The series was about a group of freedom fighters who were on the losing side of an interplanetary war, and had taken up a life of crime to keep themselves from starving to death. It was pretty grim. The music Fox chose to play during the commercials for *Firefly* was the maniacally zany song

"Walking on the Sun" by frat boy favorites Smash Mouth. Apparently, the network confused this dark riff on the depressed era of the Reconstruction for MTV's Spring Break.

I felt sympathy for them over the inevitable loss of their show, even if the show, in my mind, sucked. I sent Kiba a list of suggestions to mount a campaign that would hopefully get some much needed press attention, and maybe attract a few hundred more viewers to tune into *Firefly*.

Kiba was stressed. She was starting grad school and didn't have the time to market a television show. I have no idea what Fox's excuse was for not having time to market a television show, given that it seems to be part of their job description as a network. But they didn't. And Fox never consulted Kristen or me, but we all seemed to be on the same page as far as the pilot was concerned—the network ordered a new one, to be written in forty-eight hours. This show was so doomed.

For those of you who may be puzzled as to why a network would spend millions and millions of dollars to produce a television show and then take it out to the backlot and shoot it between the eyes, here's a little primer about how the inner financial world of broadcast television works: A network fronts an obscene amount of money to a studio full of creative-type people to produce a television series. An hour-long drama can cost about $2 million or more per episode to produce, which includes the actors' salaries, the dental plan for the guy who holds the boom, donuts, wardrobe . . . you get the picture.

Now, this may be a surprising concept, but television executives did not get into the business as a purely altruistic endeavor to entertain the unwashed masses. Networks make money by selling thirty- to sixty-second dollops of time during a program to advertisers. A TV show is just succulent bait to lure unsuspecting, hard-working Americans into watching commercials. The network promises the advertisers that a particular show will attract millions of viewers called a *demographic*. The most precious demographic is eighteen- to forty-year-old males, who supposedly have the most disposable income. So networks invest in television shows that they believe will appeal to the people who spend the most money on things like Sega games, pizza delivery, and unnecessarily large trucks. He who dies with the most toys not only wins, but also decides what the rest of us poor (dickless) jerks watch on television.

Based on the promise the network has made to the advertisers regarding the number of boys who will be watching television during a certain time period, the advertisers will shell out thousands or millions of dollars to hawk their products to the viewers. For example, a thirty-second spot during the

2004 Super Bowl cost $2.25 million. This provided drug companies with a key demographic in order to pitch Viagra and Cialis to the largest audience of limp dicks ever assembled.

The cost of making, marketing, and/or leasing a show from another studio must be even or be less than the amount of money advertisers pay for their commercial minutes in order for the show to be a success and the network to have profited from its investment. If the demographic the network promised doesn't tune into the show, the advertisers get pissed off and pull their ad dollars, feeling all disgruntled and cheated.

Now before you get all paranoid and think that the Fox network has a spycam in your house to gauge what you watch and whether you in fact have a penis and loads of disposable income, let me explain the concept of Nielsen boxes. Nielsen is a company that takes a statistical measurement of television viewers in the U.S. and abroad. There are "hundreds of thousands of Nielsen Families" according to the Nielsen website. People with Nielsen boxes and diaries decide what the rest of us watch. I've no idea how one becomes a Nielsen Family. It all seems very random, like a carload full of statisticians perform senseless drive-by shootings with spyware bullets throughout the suburbs. The Nielsen ratings are posted every morning, and advertisers can check to see whether the networks have delivered the demographics they promised.

When the network isn't delivering the promised demographic, television shows get canceled. Critical acclaim does not matter. It doesn't matter if four million twenty-year-olds with a lust for video games tuned into a show if the network promised six million of them. Your favorite television series can get axed if four Nielsen families all get together for a game of mini-golf and shut off their sets two Fridays in a row during a period called "sweeps," when Nielsen provides the most detailed data, pretty much.

It seems so unfair, but then, the only way to get completely accurate data would be to rig every television set with spyware, and then millions of paranoid Americans would switch their televisions to either PBS or C-SPAN and break the remote in an effort to conceal their late-night Cinemax guilty pleasures.

I don't know how many people were actually watching the first episode of *Firefly*. I have no idea what sort of audience share was promised to the advertisers. Whatever it was, it wasn't making good on the network's gamble. According to the Nielsen data, of the millions of people who tuned in, about half of them got bored after the first half hour and changed the channel. Perhaps to something scintillating on

Cinemax. It didn't matter to me much, because as I said, I thought the show sucked.

And then the script came in the mail.

It was October, Kristen's birthday was a couple of days away, and one of *Firefly*'s producers sent her a signed script: "Hope you keep watching for as long as we've got. Love, Tim."

Damn. GUILT.

Kristen and I hold a special place in our hearts for this particular producer, Tim Minear, who had been so kind to us back when he was working on one of our favorite shows, *Angel*. Kristen is the webmaster of Tim's fan site, TimMinear.net. She developed a friendship with Tim, and earned a place in his heart what with the site and non-crazy attitude about his work. He knew we both hated *Firefly*—we panned it in reviews on blogs and message boards. He loved us anyway. We hadn't really stopped to consider that Tim loved this show—it was as much his baby as it was Joss Whedon's. Because our love for Tim was huge and ferocious, we decided to put our shoulders to the wheel and try to save *Firefly*.

Fortunately, just as we were beginning to gather troops throughout fandom, an episode of *Firefly* aired that was actually—stunningly—*good*. It was penned by our Tim and was a uniquely nonlinear episode of television reminiscent of the noir submarine classic *Das Boot*. It was the dark, twisted, filet-of-brain kind of television Kristen and I had expected from the beginning of the series, and we were so relieved. It's much easier to try and save a show when you actually give a shit about it.

I called Joss Whedon's production company, Mutant Enemy, and informed them that we were going to try and save *Firefly*. Our plan was to do Fox's job, and actually market the show. Saving a show is hard work. It requires many hours of sitting at a non-ergonomically sound desk in front of a computer. We needed help. We needed an army. We needed $3,000.

Kristen and I have a history of running fan-funded ads in support of the television shows we love, including Stand-up for Buffy, Give Buffy an Emmy, and Congratulations on 100 Episodes of Buffy. It's a hobby. It keeps us off the streets. Our shared history as Mutant Enemy's head cheerleaders meant that the people at Whedon's production company would take our calls and give us anything we needed, no questions asked.

We researched who had reviewed *Firefly* and which reviewers panned it. We researched which companies were advertising on the series and kept a running log of them. We started designing a full-page ad for *Firefly* to run in *Daily Variety,* an industry trade magazine. At some point, I called Conan O'Brien and Craig Kilborn to see if either would like to interview Joss Whedon about the show. I may have over-stepped some boundaries.

Mutant Enemy sent us a screener for another not-unbrilliant episode of *Firefly*. We made copies to send to reviewers who hated the pilot episode, begging them to take a second look at the show and write another review. Fans can do what networks and production companies cannot. We can grovel. We don't have to worry about image, because the mainstream media already thinks we're losers. The best we can hope for is to appear to be endearing losers. Kristen and I were like little Shirley Temple Matchstick Girls with coal-smudged faces, shaking a tin cup full of VHS tapes and pleading with *Entertainment Weekly*'s Ken Tucker, "Please, kind sir, I'm starving and have nits, won't you write something nice about this television show?"

While we had a lot of leeway in what we could do to try and advertise the series, we had to be very careful not to reveal that Mutant Enemy was helping us in any way. There could be no appearance of impropriety. Years before, Kristen had campaigned hard to get the WB network to air the season three finale of *Buffy the Vampire Slayer*. The network had canceled the airing of the finale because Buffy the fictional slayer blew up her fictional high school, and the real-life Columbine shootings were still so recent. Since the network execs thought that the cult TV audience couldn't tell the difference between the Trenchcoat Mafia and Sarah Michelle Gellar, they thought it would be a PR nightmare to air the episode.

Whatever. Then-WB network head Jamie Kellner admitted in an internet chat that he never actually viewed the finale before making his decision. So Kristen raised funds and purchased a full-page ad in *Daily Variety* asking Kellner to pull his head out of his bloated ass and air the episode. The ad was titled "Stand Up for Buffy." The network accused *Buffy*'s producers of buying the ad themselves, which seemed an effort by WB executives to dismiss the audience's ire as nonexistent. By the time the WB got around to airing the finale, thousands of fans had already seen it through the most massive online tape-trading tree ever assembled. The episode had aired in Canada, and our friends to the North took pity upon us and sent copies out *en masse*.

We didn't want any accusations of insider orchestrations to happen with the *Firefly* campaign. It was hugely important for the advertisers and network to know that there was a growing, devoted fan base willing to spend an obscene amount of cash to keep the show on the air. The trouble was that Kristen and I weren't sure if the fandom was all that devoted, and even if they were we didn't know if we could get them to understand what we were doing and trust us enough to send us money and follow our lead. Since we really needed cash to fund the campaign, we decided that it'd be faster to sell something than to beg for trust.

So I called over to the show and asked for some signed scripts, T-shirts, props, anything at all that could be auctioned on eBay to raise funds.

Three scripts and a T-shirt brought in about $1,200. We were on our way. Since we couldn't tell the fans that we were talking to people at the show almost daily, it was a huge struggle to get them to follow our game plan.

Kristen and I were deeply entrenched in the *Buffy* and *Angel* fandoms for years and everyone who actively participated in those online fandoms knew us and trusted us. People who hated us would still trust us with their PINs and would possibly cosign for us on car loans. We always did what we said were going to do, and gave any leftover cash to charity, never taking a dime for ourselves.

But *Firefly* was a new show with a new fandom, completely green to the ways of internet communities. They were just discovering that there was such a thing as internet fandom, that Trekkies didn't own all the stock in television obsession.

And so when Kristen and I burst through their door babbling about our game plan for saving the show and, oh yeah, please send us all your money, the fans greeted us with skepticism and occasional hostility. It was understandable but terribly frustrating because we needed to mobilize them fast. The network had ordered only thirteen episodes of *Firefly* to be produced, nine shy of a full season. The Nielsen ratings were dismal. We knew this would make it easy for the network to pull the plug on the show at any time.

The main goal was always to get one more episode on the air. We needed the gamble the network made on *Firefly* to bear fruit. If the show could grab enough Nielsen families, *Firefly* would turn a profit, and they'd hang on for another episode. One episode at a time. The goal was to try to build the audience through word of mouth.

Have you ever read Dr. Seuss's *Horton Hears a Who!*? It's a story about an elephant holding a dandelion upon which a tiny planet populated by tiny people rests. The tiny people need to make sure the folks in Horton's world can hear them, and know that they're alive and well, or Horton will be forced to drop the dandelion in a vat of boiling oil. All the tiny people gather up and scream, "WE ARE HERE! WE ARE HERE! WE ARE HERE! WE ARE HERE!" Eventually, they are heard at the eleventh hour, and the dandelion is saved.

We appealed to the fan base, asking them to do something simple and inexpensive; send the network and advertisers postcards with their demographic info listed on it. We told them to be their own Nielsen boxes. The cast and crew of *Firefly* were told that no one was watching, that they were playing to an empty house. In our effort to write our own tale, *FOX President Gail Berman Hears a Fandom,* and to try to save our show from being dumped in the Cauldron of Cancellation, we got fans to send eight thousand postcards to the network in just two weeks.

Our *Daily Variety* ad was published December 9, 2002. We thanked the network heads for green-lighting the series, we thanked the cast and crew, and we thanked each advertiser by name. The ad was passed around to the cast and crew, who up until then were under the impression that no one was watching their work. Cranky Hollywood industry folk were abuzz about the classiness of this particular fan effort.

We were inspired. We seemed to be making progress. The network was our oyster.

Less than a week later, *Firefly* was canceled.

We got word from Tim Minear at one of the message boards we haunted during the campaign.

Tim Minear. December 13, 2002, 1:28:30 a.m. PST

Hey, guys.

First off, wanted to say out loud to all what a brill ad that was in *Variety*. We were all impressed and moved. Not only was it dang nice, the doing of the thing, but it was really classy and smart.

Okay. Sigh.

We did get word tonight, Fox won't be ordering any new eps. That translates to "cancelled." We will finish shooting the ep now in production (I'm directing, in fact Joss came down to the set to break the bad news to cast and crew – we wrapped early, but are back at it in the am), we'll finish post on all eps, and Fox says they're going to somehow air all eps. One expects with giant banner ads over them for Meet My Rich Phoney Sex Date or whatever unreality series they've got up their, er, sleeves.

That morning, I took up a small collection to send flowers over to the set for the crew members who had just found themselves pink-slipped two weeks before Christmas. We were completely deflated for about thirty seconds. When the Rapture comes, you want Kristen and me on your side.

The next day, we made calls to find out if Mutant Enemy was going to shop the show to another network. As it turned out, they were taking their pitch to UPN. So we pulled a U-turn and crashed the campaign through the network's front door. Kristen posted the new directions before our fandom army had a chance to go AWOL.

Kristen. December 13, 2002, 3:36:31 p.m. PST

Attention, K-Mart Shoppers . . . I mean, Buffistas . . .

Okay, we have a direction to point you in. We like to call this direction UPN.

What we need are postcards by the truckload going to Les Moonves and Dawn Tarnofsky-Ostroff. You can send any kind of postcards you'd like to but we thought it would be a nice touch if the cards had a certain uniformity.

There is now a PDF up at [the Firefly Support site]. It's an 8.5 x 11 sheet of postcards that feature the *Variety* ad. You can print the document onto cardstock, cut them into fours and, voila, four handy postcards . . . On the back, let them know how much you enjoyed the show while it was on FOX, and how eager you are for it to find a home with UPN. Keep things upbeat and positive, so they'll know what classy fans Joss and his crew will be bringing to the network! Some ideas for things to mention: your favorite episode, why the show moves you, why you think the show has potential, etc.

Our two catchwords now are: VOLUME and SPEED.

We need a lot of postcards on their desks really damn fast.

Thanks guys!

Kristen got a call from Tim Minear's assistant that week. We were invited to the set to watch the final episode filming. I got to sit in the pilot's chair of the spaceship set and be a complete fangurl dork, punching the buttons, steering, making VROOOOM noises. I made a complete jackass out of myself and loved every second of it. It was an important thing to be able to touch the thing we were so desperately trying to save. Now I know how those fuzzy-headed environmentalists feel when they swim with dolphins or chain themselves to falling redwoods.

The fans were furious about the cancellation, and it appeared as though our grassroots campaign to rally the fandom had caught fire. As more people jumped on the Save *Firefly* bandwagon, it got increasingly hard to steer. I blame *Roswell*.

Roswell was a sci-fi show on the WB that received quite a bit of publicity when fans sent thousands of bottles of Tabasco sauce to the network in an attempt to save the show from cancellation. The sexy teenage aliens on *Roswell* had hard-ons for hot sauce, so it was all very symbolic. *Roswell* didn't get canceled, the fans rejoiced, and a legend was born. Every fan campaign to save a show since has been left with this *Roswell* legacy that says if you flood the network with whatever weird object used for product placement, your show will be saved from cancellation.

This is further proof that too many confuse brainstorms with shitstorms. The *Roswell* pickup was more complex than Tabasco, but the show sure did get a lot of press from the fiery condiment.

Fans wanted to send apples to the network after an episode of *Firefly* aired in which apples were containers for tiny bombs that would blow one's head off at first bite. Another suggested sending millions of blue latex gloves, as worn by the creepy villains on *Firefly*. Post 9/11, sending containers of anything unsolicited to a huge media conglomerate is not such a good idea, though. We needed to steer the fans away from sending crates of apples, boxes of rubber gloves, or mailing their own ears (à la Van Gogh) to the network lest we spark a huge anthrax panic that would cause the network to evacuate the offices.

Suggestions become actions very quickly. How to put the kibosh on such suggestions without appearing an evil tyrant hell-bent on destroying someone's dream of good intentions is not my forte. This is what I posted to a message board after Fox canned *Firefly* and we were appealing to UPN to pick the show up:

> Do not send gloves, apples, underwear, flowers,
> finger paintings, tabasco, pixie sticks, chocolates,

or any object, of any kind, to anyone.

Send postcards. That's all. You want to do more? Send a postcard to your affiliate station. More than that? Write a letter to the editor of your favorite magazine or newspaper.

But that's it.

The fans are not in a position to force, intimidate, or convince anyone to pick up this show.

Joss/Mutant Enemy (ME) is in that position. We are supporting that position. That is all.

Every object that you send will be perceived as threatening, and make a bad impression. It will hinder, not help.

UPN and FOX will have no friggin clue what blue gloves mean. They won't. They won't see the symbolism, and even so, what IS the symbolism? Think about who wears the blue gloves, and whether those characters are hostile.

Send postcards, write to affiliates and media outlets, and for the love of all that is good and holy, do not do anything that makes us look like asswipes.

I know intentions are good. I understand and am happy that people want to do more. You're doing enough. We've shown the network that there is heavy interest in the show. Now Joss/ME has to show the network that it would be profitable for them.

Either he will succeed or fail. But NO ONE is going to do something that may cause a friggin evacuation of UPN's offices.

We're not PICKETING. We're not PROTESTING.

Those things make us look like we've got several screws loose.

So far, we're bright and funny and loyal. Let's keep it that way.

I guess you could say I lost my shit completely. We were only a couple of weeks from closing up shop on the *Firefly* campaign, and I had been taking everything entirely too seriously for two months. My brain hurt. I wanted my life back. My email inbox had been bursting at the cyberseams for weeks with zany suggestions involving crates of irradiated fruit and accusations of being a starfucker. Kristen talked me down from the ledge and reminded me that this was supposed to be more hobby, less crusade.

What began as a love letter to a favorite writer turned into an insanely epic and ridiculous drama that sucked my brain out of my ear and regurgitated it on the bathroom floor. I'm sure this sort of drama happens on smaller scales at PTA bake sales and town hall meetings about the importance of newly-placed stop signs across America.

It's absurdly easy to hook one's claws into a cause and hang on long after it stops bucking and lies down dead on the pavement. Onlookers ask if there isn't anything better you can do with your time, and all you can do is hiss and bare your fangs and make nonsensical arguments, inflating importance and meaning until the cause is bloated and deformed, unrecognizable.

But it was important to me, and about four million other weekly viewers who tuned in every Friday for an hour of escapism, and the thousands who flocked to message boards to discuss the thing that gave them some measure of happiness for a little while. It was certainly important to the caterers and actors and production assistants who made their living pulling *Firefly* together every week. Maybe my time could have been better spent protesting the anal electrocution of minks by hurling paintballs at elite models wearing fur-lined panties. That certainly seems more noble a cause than protesting the cancellation of a cult television program.

A couple of years after the cancellation, Joss Whedon managed to produce a feature film based on the series, called

Serenity. The film was critically acclaimed, but barely made a dime. The marketing campaign for *Serenity* laid it on thick with the story of the fans' dedication making the movie possible. Every one of those commercials kicked me in the ass with the boot of irony.

I look at TV the way some people look at their neighborhood pub: It's the way I escape the monotony of everyday life, the daily typing of memos, and cleaning of the cat's litter box. In the end, *Firefly* gave me some measure of joy in my otherwise painfully dull life. The campaign kept my head busy, kept me focused on something interesting outside of my tiny world. It meant a great deal to some folks I adore, it provided me with some sort of clear goal that wasn't about expense reports or choosing the right 401(k) stocks.

And I got to pilot a spaceship.

Celebrity Pussy

One day while meditating (slacking) in front of my computer at work, I got a call from the mighty Joss Whedon's office. It was Kern, one of Whedon's assistants, and he sounded mildly desperate.

"Do you know anyone who wants a cat?"

In my world, this question sets off the same firing of defense neurons that happens when a stranger on a bus asks, "Would you like to attend our church's open house on Sunday?" Any answer other than "yes" is going to set off a conversation in which I will be assaulted with guilt. It's hard to say no to an animal, when you know the alternative is that the critter will likely be gassed at the local shelter or live a miserable life in a tiny cage being poked at every week on Pet Adoption Day in front of a grocery store at a strip mall.

I have a cat, a rescue named Ruby who hates other cats the way I hate other people. I'm content with Ruby, and would no more bring home another cat than she would bring home another human. Mutual respect, that. I thought of Ruby and said I couldn't take the cat, but I'd ask around and get back to him if anyone wanted the soon-to-be-evicted feline.

Kern pleaded that this was a hugely time-sensitive issue, since the couple who owned the animal had just had a baby who was recently diagnosed with a severe allergy to cats.

My brain is slow on the uptake in the morning. It took me a minute to remember that Joss and his wife just had a baby. So I asked, "Whose cat is it?"

He quickly, nervously replied, "A friend, why do you need to know?" Defensive.

I stifled laughter. It was ten a.m. on a workday. He was determined to find a home for this cat and wasn't using the silent, private communication method of web-based email. I'm an assistant, I know all the signs. This was an assigned task. This was his boss's cat. I'm unsure why Kern was reluctant to tell me the truth about the cat. Maybe he thought that by not admitting it, he had some sort of plausible deniability thing going in case Joss would later waterboard him for cat adoption intel.

Since there was a sick child involved, I let him know that I had a friend who ran a nonprofit cat rescue who might have some alternatives given the gravity of the situation.

In the same microsecond it took to hang up the phone, I was instant messaging my partner in fandom follies, Kristen, "Dude, have I got a story for YOU."

As it turned out, Kristen and I did have a mutual friend, Amanda, who was trying to convince her husband, Brad, to let her adopt a cat. Brad was on the fence about the whole thing, but Kristen said she'd make the call and see if the cat's shiny background would help clinch the deal.

Meanwhile, Kern called me every day to ask what the progress was on finding a home for the cat-that-didn't-belong-to-Joss Whedon. It was clear that the bastard had delegated this task to me. I didn't tell anyone outside my Small Circle of Confidants the truth about who the alleged cat owner was. I understood the twinge of fear in Kern's voice. It'd be terribly easy for me to go forth to the internet and ask if anyone wanted Joss's cat. I'd have a thousand emails in my inbox from sycophantic assholes who can't take care of their own personal hygiene, let alone a cat. Some of these assholes would probably try to eBay the cat with a bold, all caps description like

THIS CAT HAS PROBABLY SEEN JOSS NAKED AND IS A RARE ONE-OF-A-KIND-ITEM!

The winning bidder would spend $2,000 and have the cat shipped to Utah, where he would marry and try to procreate with the cat, or eat the cat's brains in an effort to try and absorb its memories.

I shared Kern's concerns. As much as I love my fandom, as much as I am prone to fiercely advocate for them, I have no illusions about the fact that some of them are batshit crazy. I also got the feeling that had the owner-who-was-not-Joss known that I, Queen Fandom, was involved in this, that Kern would have been strung up by his balls. The people who make the shows we love are actual human beings and should be treated accordingly. It's my understanding of these things, in addition to the fact that I'm a sucker, that gave Kern the incentive to call me in the first place.

The week wore on, and the calls became more frequent as Kristen tried to get in touch with the possible adoptive cat owners, who were traveling for work. I told Kern to tell his "friend" that we should perhaps go the no-kill shelter route, which was the Worst Case Scenario option. The cat-that-didn't-belong-to-Joss was well-loved, and it was clear that this was a painful matter to the owner-who-wasn't-Joss. The goal was to find a decent, loving home.

I told Kern to fax me the cat's vet records to speed up the process of getting the cat into a good shelter, or to give to the new owners in the event that our friend Amanda succeeded in warming her husband toward adoption.

Kern freaked the fuck out. Why did I need vet records? It's a cat! The cat is healthy! Argh! Kern was upset that his plausible deniability was evaporating. If I had the vet records, I'd also have proof of who owned the cat, and perhaps could use that proof to blackmail Kern for an autographed Buffy lunchbox or something. I guess.

I gently explained that a good shelter wouldn't take the cat unless it had vaccination and health records. A good owner would want to know when the cat's shots needed updating. Begrudgingly, he faxed the cat's vet records . . . with the owner's name and address blacked out in magic marker.

Since I had called Joss Whedon's office so many times in the past to ask for help with different fandom related projects, and they always graciously gave me whatever support I needed, I felt an obligation to help Kern. Return the Karma, you know? But with the flip out over the vet records and the scrubbed address, I was losing patience. It seemed to not occur to Kern that I was actually doing his job for him, and it was weirdly inappropriate for him to be placing any sort of pressure on me to do so. If I didn't feel so grateful to his boss for all the entertaining television, I would have told Kern to shove the cat up his ass.

Amanda called right before the last straw was about to spontaneously combust and said her husband was so tickled by the whole story that he couldn't refuse her cat need any longer. She'd be driving down to L.A. on business, from her home in San Francisco, in a couple of days and would be able to pick up the cat-that-did-not-belong-to-Joss.

I had to give Kern a full description of Amanda and her husband, what they did for a living, whether they owned their home or rented, how I knew them, what sort of neighborhood they lived in, and why they wanted a cat. He stopped just shy of asking for a urine sample. I was irritated by the interrogation. The phone call went on for about a half hour. Once so desperate to find anyone slightly less insane than Jim Jones to take the kitty, he was suddenly grilling me to ensure these were quality adopters. I was wondering if I'd have to administer a Rosarch test with inkblots shaped like rubber mice. I wasn't going to call Amanda and ask, "Are you now, or have you ever been a catnip user?" I did find myself lying about the square footage of their home, and making some crap up about their income. Seriously, he wanted to know what sort of jobs they held. I was cycling between amused and irritated. I was sitting at work, being interviewed on the quality of my friends, and their ability to fill a dish with kibble every morning.

Kern would probably be interrogated by his boss and needed backup information about how it all went down, leaving the fandom part out of it, and I understood it. It didn't make the whole thing any less annoying.

Kern dropped the cat off at Kristen's since she brokered the deal. We all felt like we were receiving stolen property, or a kilo of heroin, instead of the soft and friendly sweetheart of a kitty who showed up at the door with a bagful of toys and treats. I kept expecting an envelope stuffed with hush money to be delivered to me at my office via some courier with peculiar facial scars. Sadly, this never happened.

The cat now lives a content, spoiled life in a pretty little home in San Francisco. In order to protect her identity, or maybe just because it's an apt description of the cat, her name has been changed from Vinnie to Meow Meow Kitty. The cat doesn't seem to give a shit what she's called as long as her new owners pick her up and scratch her ears three thousand times a day.

About a year and a half later, I was throwing a charity party at the Century City Plaza. It was the first time since the clandestine cat transfer took place that Kern, Kristen, Amanda, and I all happened to be in the same place. I grabbed Amanda and dragged her into the Green Room to confront Kern once and for all. I looked Kern in the eye and asked him point-blank to confirm who Meow Meow Kitty's previous owners were. Either softened by booze or time, he relented the coyness. "Yeah, it was Joss's cat."

Amanda then took the opportunity to describe the litany of health issues that came with the cat, beginning with fleas and ending with some sort of dental issue. Meow Meow Kitty was more of a fixer-upper than had been advertised.

In hindsight, this was the first instance of the more equitable relationship I eventually came to know with the mighty Joss Whedon's office. Every time I see Joss at a signing or premiere or something, I want to tell him that his cat is healthy and loved. I mean, I'd want to know how my cat was doing. I'd want to know that she was safe and happy if I had to give her away to strangers. But I say nothing, because I don't know how he'd feel about that. Maybe he misses Vinnie, but has made peace with the choice he made to spare his son's respiratory system from the dander. Better to keep quiet.

Kern later went to work for a different producer, a colleague of Joss's. He called me a few months after getting the new gig, seemingly just to chat about what's new in my world. We talked about our jobs and our lives, about television, whether he was any closer to his dream of producing. Joss's cult television dynasty was over, and my role as intermediary between fandom and objects-of-fandom-devotion was winding down. It was interesting to get a call that wasn't about one of us needing help on a task, just a "checking-in" conversation of sorts between colleagues on the fandom continuum. There seemed to be little to say, anymore. The conversation dissipated quickly, and so we both sort of let the small talk wander toward the END button on our cell phones. Just as we were getting to the "Well, maybe I'll see you around . . ." part of the call, Kern interjected with one last question before clicking off, "Hey, Do you know anyone who wants a dog?"

High Stakes 2004 Fundraiser for Kerry/Edwards

In the interest of full disclosure: I'm a lifelong Democrat, and I voted for John Kerry. That said, I briefly considered voting for Bush while at Joss Whedon's fundraiser for Kerry, High Stakes 2004, so named for the abject terror we Democrats felt about a possible four more years of Shrub, and a nod to Buffy's weapon of choice. Get it? Stake? Har. It's not that I don't have a lot of love for Joss Whedon or John Kerry; it's just that I'm infuriatingly contrary. If I'm in a room full of people who all agree that something rocks, I must be the asshole pontificating on why that thing sucks ass. I am that jerk.

The fundraiser was at Cinespace, a restaurant/movie theatre in Hollywood. Celebrity guests included *Buffy* alumni Alyson

Hannigan, Nicholas Brendon, Amber Benson, Adam Busch, Danny Strong, and Tom Lenk. *Angel* was represented by Alexis Denisof, J. August Richards, and Amy Acker. *Firefly* was also in the house, personified by the gregarious Nathan Fillion.

Here's how it all went down:

Rumors had been spreading for weeks that Joss Whedon was going to host some sort of fundraiser for the Kerry campaign. So I called over to Mutant Enemy and got the scoop from Joss's assistant. "Ah, Allyson, I was gonna call you . . ." Joss needed a password to a site and some hints at where to post info about the event. Since I'm fandom's bitch, I obliged.

I found out that Joss was going to participate in a confer- ence call to raise money for the Kerry campaign. Joss's fans could call in to a sort of party line on Sunday around two p.m. and talk to the man (Joss, not Kerry) for the low price of a $35 donation to Kerry/Edwards. Bush supporters had to pay the higher price of abandoning all their principles by making a donation to the Kerry campaign.

Eventually, the conference call evolved into a party, where fans could pay $50 to both listen to *and* watch Joss talk to other fans on the phone through a little glass window in the sound booth. It was an opportunity for Joss to trade in his celebrity for a cause he cared about, and an opportunity for fans to spend a bit of time hanging out with Joss in a far more intimate setting than a convention.

I didn't pay any money for any it (as Joss's assistant reminded me after I bitched about a $9 gin and tonic). I got a VIP pass to get in due to shilling the event on the net. I would ordinarily feel a great degree of guilt for getting in free to a fundraiser, but I'm from Massachusetts, and therefore have been supporting Kerry since birth. I figured we were even, John and me.

And so when I arrived I was whisked upstairs to the party, where some dude who does press for Kerry was waiting to shake my hand. I asked him if there was a place for press to set up, and he said press wasn't going to be allowed in the party. I was not allowed to take notes or record conversations with anyone, because "Josh wants to keep it loose and informal."

I didn't know who Josh was or why he was busting my nut, because I had been told by Joss's office that press would be welcome. I wondered if it meant that the security guard was going to confiscate my pen, so I asked if I could still come in. Press Dude said that I was of course welcome; I was on Josh's VIP list!

It occurred to me that he meant to say, "Joss."

I leaned in and whispered in his ear, "It's *Josssss*."

He replied, "I have a lisp!"

But lisp has an "s" in it, and he totally didn't lisp that word. So in addition to being pissed off about not being able to write anything down, I was also obsessing about the lisp charade. I immediately called my editor to lament. And then I called everyone else I had ever met to tell them I was a hanger-on in a Top Seekrit political fundraiser with minor celebrities whom my mom has never heard of.

I wandered uncomfortably through the room, taking pictures of actors chatting with fans while news footage of Kerry played in the background on theatre screens. There was no sound, just John Kerry's enormous noggin on flat screens strewn haphazardly throughout the room. Kerry could have been talking about healthcare or monkey balls, I wouldn't know. If I wasn't already reading *Salon*, *National Review*, *The New York Times*, *The Washington Post*, and dozens of bloggers across the net, I'd have been no more educated on John Kerry by attending this fundraiser. But then, fundraisers aren't so much about educating people about a cause; they're about getting you to contribute to a cause you already believe in. Celebrity fundraisers attract believers and starfuckers alike, and as long as they all put a little money in the pot, it doesn't really matter why you came. I was there as a starfucker/believer, but the only person who got my money was the bartender.

Eventually, the announcement came over the loudspeaker that Joss was going to start talking to other fans on the phone. I can't fully explain how bizarre it was. Joss was shoved into a small room not much bigger than the phone booth that whisks Doctor Who through all sorts of weird dimensions. Joss was shoehorned in with several other people like minor-celebrity veal. One could peek through a small glass window in the booth and see Joss earnestly listening to something the audience couldn't hear. A moderator read questions to Joss that were sent in by people around the country who had agreed to throw Kerry fundraiser parties.

And so everyone stood around, frozen, staring at the floor or the wall, listening to Joss answer questions on the phone. Some crowded around the little window to watch. Others quietly checked the flash on their cameras and succumbed to attention deficit disorder until the flash went off in their faces. Maybe that just happened to me.

This is what a report looks like when no one lets you have a pen so you can concentrate on taking notes:

Moderator: Some person who lives somewhere wants to know if Sunnydale County votes Republican or Democrat.

Allyson's Brain: Oooh, that's an adorable question, I must concentrate so I remember it.

Joss Whedon: Sunnydale is a place where the people in charge want the citizens to keep their heads in the sand . . .

Allyson's Brain: Hey, Amber Benson and Adam Busch are still dating. She has shiny hair. Shit, I'm not concentrating.

Joss Whedon: So, no, I'm not going to write or direct *X-Men 3,* because I realized no one asked me to do that and if you show up and start directing a movie when no one asked you to . . .

Allyson's Brain: Shit, I totally missed the Sunnydale answer. I wonder if this will take the full two hours. Amber Benson has shiny hair.

Moderator: A random person from some town wants to know if you would consider doing a Faith series now that Eliza Dusku's show is canceled.

All I can remember is he answered that he'd love to if she wanted to, and then I became confused because I remembered someone telling me Joss didn't want to so much be doing TV anymore, which was later confirmed in *Daily Variety.* He cut his contract with 20th and can't develop anything for TV for like, a year.

This went on for some time. Eventually it ended and I went out for a smoke, where I saw Herc, a writer from the website AintItCoolNews.com. Herc, as it turns out, was the ringleader of the event. He's a tall red-headed guy who wears dark sunglasses and has a talent for finding a way to take up as much space as possible. I introduced myself.

He thought my name was Alyssa. I corrected him. He said, "Allyson? Are you my assistant?"

"No. I am not your fucking assistant, jackass," I think, but do not say.

He said, "There are a lot of Allysons here."

Whatever. I asked again if I could take his picture. He said that it's supposed to be sort of a mystery as to what he really looks like—it's a thing. I smiled sweetly and played the mousy fangurl card and told him he could cover his face with his jacket. I thought that if he was so concerned with keeping up his cyber-Batman identity, he should invest in a burka, especially if he was going to hold court at Hollywood fundraisers. He let me take the picture.

There was a long line to talk to Joss, and I got in it, thinking that maybe I could get a question in on the sly. Joss was taking time with every fan, posing for pictures, having real conversations, I presume. I made some calls, watched Kerry's enormous head mouth words on a screen, and then it was my turn.

"Hi, I'm Allyson."

Joss registered no recognition.

I wasn't sure where to go next.

"Hi Joss, I worked on three enormous charity fundraisers in your honor. You were at a couple of them. I worked on an Emmy consideration campaign for *Buffy*. I ran the campaign to save *Firefly* with my best friend and your webmaster, I wrote that *Variety* ad you liked so much. I organized the fans and sent you a basket full of children's books and the donation to First Book in your son's honor when he was born. I'm now working with the Army to send $4,000 worth of *Firefly* DVDs to the troops abroad as a donation from your fans. I found a home for your cat when you discovered your baby was allergic. I've had two different television crews cover parties to celebrate one of your television shows and I've met you five thousand times AND YOU NEVER REMEMBER WHO I AM."

But I didn't actually say that, because, really, why would he know who I am? I'm a psychotic Big Name Fan weirdo who has dedicated too much time to this guy's work. Do I really want him to remember me? Sure I do. But he's never going to remember.

So I just said, "I'm going to hug you."

As it turns out, Joss is corporeal. He's sort of squishy and not at all godlike, as some fans would lead you to believe.

I shook his hand and said, "I wrote the *Variety* ad to save *Firefly*." (Notice the pathetic nature of the statement, just begging for some recognition.)

He said, "Thank you."

I smiled, asked if I could take his picture, and he obliged. He leaned in so I could ask a question and I said, "I don't have anything else, I'm just going to hug you again."

And then he leaned over and kissed me tenderly on my cheek, and I went back to the smoking lounge to call a neo-con friend and whine, "Joss has no idea who I am, I'm voting for Bush."

Then there were closing statements. Press Dude who wouldn't let me write anything got on stage and thanked Josh. He reminded us that it was very important that young women vote. Okey doke, Press Dude. Joss followed up with some quips about not voting for a man who thinks the Presidency was a birthday gift from his daddy. Then it was over, and I went to find Joss's assistant to thank him for inviting me. He was talking to Press Dude and asked, "Have you met Allyson?"

I told Press Dude that I was there to write for Popgurls.com, a web magazine whose readership is tens of thousands of young women.

He replied, "Well, there's a lot of single guys here!"

I had no idea how to respond.

He said that he was concerned about press interviewing people and having a celebrity say something sketchy that could wind up in the news so close to the election.

I really wouldn't want to be responsible for misquoting Tom Lenk and costing Kerry the election, not when Press Dude was there to point out the fine array of men with whom I could possibly score a quickie.

Like I said, I'm a lifelong Democrat, a hardcore liberal. It wouldn't really matter to me whether Joss was a liberal or conservative or one of those Larouche people who troll for signatures outside my grocery store at election time. It wouldn't make me admire his work any less, nor would his views have any influence on mine. I have, however, given some thought to Whedon's conservative fans, and how they must have felt very left out of this opportunity to meet their heroes. I mean, it was a really relaxed environment despite a few clusterfuck moments here and there. The fans were all lovely and kind and patient, offering to take photos for other people, no shoving or rudeness of any kind did I witness. Just smiling and laughing and hugging. The celebrity guests were gracious and patient. There were times when they stood alone, contently eating crudités and people-watching. It was a lovely, intimate event that was surely of interest to any fan of any political persuasion.

But, given the nature of the event, any conservative fan whose gut principles lie on the right side of the line in the sand just couldn't attend. No one says life is fair, but as Joss said while talking to someone on the phone, he wants his work to appeal to all people. It's just difficult, sometimes, to separate the man from his work, especially if you're a fan of both the man *and* his work. I get that this was something important to him, and support his right to get on a soapbox and cry foul if he feels that is righteous. The nature of celebrity is that you get an especially large soapbox, microphone, and mixer to help spread your message.

As late as it was in the election season, this sort of event is strictly to raise funds. It wouldn't have actually changed any minds that had been set, and at best, possibly could have inspired a few more people to vote who may have been apathetic about it. So that's okay.

At worst, Joss could have traded in a great deal of the capital he built in the last ten years for the amount of money to pay for a thirty second attack ad in Ohio, and I wonder if that was worth alienating a truckload of his conservative fans who probably felt more than a bit unwelcome at this particular party.

I'm not quite sure how I feel about the whole thing. As a spectator, I was entertained. As a writer, it was reasonably interesting subject matter. As a fan, it was a cool opportunity to ogle my heroes. As a voter, it didn't really matter to me at all whether Joss Whedon voted Kerry or Bush. He could have been a Conservative Christian Pat Buchanan supporter and I would have liked him more if he had remembered my name. Political leanings are such a tiny part of who we are, in total. Celebrity doesn't lend any more credence to a message. It just makes the message a little louder, and means the message probably comes with fancy cheese cubes.

Imposter!

Sitting Shiva (which is the Jewish version of an Irish wake, but with cake instead of beer) after my grandfather was buried, I found myself engaged in bizarre conversations with people loosely related to me. My aunt Roxanne called me from across the room, "Allyson! Come tell Auntie So-and-So about your friend Timmy who makes television shows!" "Allyson, come tell Cousin What's-Her-Name about your book!" "Come tell us all about the parties you throw for celebrities!"

And so I went and told stories about writing, that the TV people were all very nice and drove expensive cars, and that publicists are almost always assholes. Their assumption is that I do something Hollywoodish for a living; that I'm on some network's payroll. But I've never made a dime off of any sort of fandom activity. I've yet to turn a profit on a fundraiser, and no one pays me for writing reviews. When I got an offer to be paid for writing this book, I assumed Ashton Kutcher would jump out of my bathroom at any moment to tell me I've been *Punk'd.*

My day job is processing travel reports for physicists in a research laboratory. One day while I was sitting at my desk, minding my own business, a very sweet physicist complimented me on the music streaming from iTunes, and suggested a music book called *Lost in the Grooves* by David Smay. I beamed, "David and his wife Jacqueline are my friends. I'll tell him you suggested his book to me; he'll be tickled." The physicist cocked his head and looked at the floor, brow furrowed. I got the impression that he thought I was lying.

This happens to me fairly often. It's why I cringed every time my aunt proudly introduced me as some Hollywood insider to tangential family members. At least a third of them get that same furrowed look on their faces, like I'm snowing them. It's because to them, television and film production might as well take place in a hothouse on the moon. It's a far-away place where real, living, breathing, working people don't really exist except on tourist trolleys.

I'm terribly paranoid about people believing that I'm a fraud. It's my biggest fear right after spiders, but before zombies who can run really fast. As it turns out, there's an entire syndrome (not endorsed by psychiatrists but possibly attributable to dead aliens living in our heads) related to this fear. Wikipedia.com tells me that Imposter Syndrome is a sort of paranoia which leaves high achieving individuals in a state of fear that everyone will find them out to be incompetent, that every success is attributable to luck, and that everyone around them will eventually discover that they are frauds.

> Individuals experiencing this syndrome seem unable to internalize their accomplishments. Regardless of what level of success they may have achieved in their chosen field of work or study, or what external proof they may have of their competence, they remain convinced internally that they do not deserve the success they have achieved and are really frauds.

Just so we're clear, I have a nonsensical hatred of "syndromes." Chronic Fatigue Syndrome, Battered Wife Syndrome, blah blah blah you can send me all the hate mail you want. I get pissy when every human foible is attributed to a "syndrome." You don't get to have a syndrome because you're tired. If you shiv the bastard who's been beating the piss out of you, that makes you normal. Welcome to humanity, here's your complimentary beverage.

The fear of being thought of as a fraud, or incompetent, is probably as common as that weird dream most people have about running in slow motion from some threat . . . a threat like zombies that can FloJo a mile without dropping any loose flesh. Fucking zombies.

This, of course, brings me to a recent disaster that jammed its bony thumb right into my Everyone-Will-Know-I'm-an-Incompetent-Fraud! Button: My agent asked me what other fans on the net think of my relationships, my access and connections to a small handful of the writers, assistants, producers of the television shows we love. I figured that most fans on the internet don't know who I am, and of those who do, the vast majority of them don't really care who is on my speed dial and vice versa.

To test my theory, I took a poll in my online journal. I posted a link to a couple of web communities I haunt on a regular basis, and asked my brethren in fandom to come by and let me know just what they think of me. I also opened up the anonymous commenting feature in my journal. Anonymous commenting allows unregistered, nameless users to call me a pathetic starfucker without fear of reprisal. In other words, it allowed people to tell me what they say behind my back.

Ninety-four percent of the respondents didn't really give a poop who I know. Of those who left anonymous comments, there were maybe four or five that were somewhat nasty and contemptuous . . . much less than I thought I'd get. It's a tribute to my enormous ego (or my Imposter Syndrome) that I figured dozens of people would take time out of their day to fill a balloon with accusatory bile and huck it onto my online journal.

Take this Anonymous post for example

> While I do not doubt you know Tim Minear, I do wonder how close *he* would consider your friendship. It seems to me that you 'name drop' him and [David] Fury as often as possible. This seems to be an attempt to increase your own 'rank' in fandoms. And I can't imagine a 'close friend' behaving that way. So just from an outside point of view, since I've never met you in real life, my knee-jerk assumption would be this: You know Tim Minear. Tim Minear knows you. You are probably not actually close friends if you use his fame/name as you do, or at least not to *my*

standard of what a close friend (and certainly not family) would be. And everyone has their own standards, but again, I'm going off of my own.

In various fandoms, I have come across many people who consider themselves good friends with celebrities they have only met once or had a 10 minute conversation with. Now, I don't think this is the case with you, but I do wonder if a fan can really have a good grasp on what constitutes a 'friendship' with an idol. (Anonymous post to my Livejournal, February 22, 2006)

For the next couple of weeks, I felt an almost irrepressible need to prove to Anonymous that I wasn't overstating my relationships. I was being called out as a fraud. A liar. An imposter. I was adamant in my need to defend myself. And then became hyper-aware that anything I said to defend myself would come across as, well, defensive. And then Anonymous would think I was a *defensive* fraud. It never occurred to me that I didn't actually have to give a shit about Anonymous's acidic digs. Simply because the post was negative, it must be *correct*.

I had to call Tim so he could reassure me that I wasn't imagining our entire relationship. He said, "Why would you make something like that up? I'm not even famous! You could make up something way better than me." He said I should tell Anonymous that we had a good laugh about it while soaking in a bubble bath.

In all fairness to Anonymous, I understand why he/she is cynical. On the net, anyone can make any sort of outlandish (or mundane) claim they want, and no one has much to go on to judge whether they're making shit up or not. To Anonymous, it's outlandish to think a fan can make a friend-ship work with someone he/she admires. This is puzzling. I admire all of my friends. That's sort of why I wanted to be friends with them in the first place. If I wanted unadmirable friends, I'd go hang outside the gates at San Quentin or Attica giving rides to hitchhiking parolees.

This doesn't change the fact that I was desperate for Anonymous to believe me, while being certain that Anonymous was right in everything he/she wrote. This one post, in tandem with a couple of similar posts accusing me of thinking I was special (and that I am most certainly *not* spe-cial) sent me into a tizzy, seeking validation from anyone who would listen to me whine. I needed some sort of assurance that I wasn't making up the past seven years of my life in some sort of horrid delusion of fandom grandeur.

Still, I remained convinced that it was impossible for any-one to like or respect me because I'm so obviously an incompetent asshole who has to carefully snow people into thinking I'm not a total fuckup. I couldn't internalize Tim's lovingly funny hair pats because I figured he just didn't want to hurt my feelings or something. I know. It's ridiculously neurotic. I'm not saying it makes any sense, and I understand how boring it would be if you had to listen to someone constantly beg for reassurance. I pretty much keep this neurosis to myself and pretend to be outwardly nonchalant. I'm only sharing this with you, the reader, because we're such great friends.

For my own sanity, I had to find out if the anonymous Livejournal commenters were on to something. I needed a neutral party to assure me that what Anonymous posted was untrue, that it was possible to be friends with someone whose work one admires, and that I hadn't imagined any of the connections I had made. I needed Mike Boretz.

My entire relationship to *BtVS* creator Joss Whedon exists through Mike Boretz, his assistant. There's a clear boundary between me as a fan, and Joss Whedon as the King Daddy of our fandom. If Joss loses his password at a message board, I email the password to Mike. If a bunch of fans raise money for a good cause in Joss's name, I email the news to Mike, who tells Joss, who will then let the fans know it's appreciated. But Joss doesn't know who I am, and I never developed a friendship with Mike the way I did with Tim Minear's assistant, John Gray. It tends to be purely business between Mike and me, and the business is fandom. I broke through that business boundary to ask some personal questions about our relationship on the Good Ship Fandom. It has always made me a little nervous every time I call Mike for something fandom related. I keep expecting him to tell me to stop calling, since I'm such a useless freak. Syndrome. Imposter.

But since Mike had no reason whatsoever to lie to me, or to keep up the self-flagellating fantasy in my head that every one around me is just taking pity on me or is part of some elaborate ruse of a practical joke, he was my go-to guy. What I wanted to know from Mike was if it were true that I was some sort of pathetic fandom social climber, why was it that he still took my calls?

"Why do I still take your calls? You're a good point person, and you're competent. As an assistant you have to make judgment calls about the people trying to reach your boss. You learn who you can work with and trust. You were helpful with whatever we were doing, political stuff, charity stuff. Keeping us in the know."

Talking to Mike was like microdermabrasion for my ego. He's not patient with my syndrome and just gives me his no-nonsense thoughts.

I was curious about the contention that one can't develop any sort of equitable relationship with a person whose work one admires.

Mike gave it some thought and replied, "Well, if you're objectifying someone you can't have a mutual friendship, because you can't see them as a real person. But it's not . . . I've seen it happen. Joss is a huge fan of Stephen Sondheim. He recently got the chance to meet him and over time they've developed a friendship. There's a difference between admiring someone and being obsessed with someone. Under the right circumstances anything is possible. I hear celebrities are people too."

This all made me feel a tiny bit better about Anonymous's accusations that I was overstating a relationship for my own weird personal fannish gain. But I still found myself in this weird place where I just couldn't believe him when he said I was competent. I called Jenny Lynn for a second opinion. Jenny ran the office for Joss's production company, Mutant Enemy. She's the person who took the brunt of my phone calls back when Kristen and I tried to save *Firefly*, which is a completely different chapter in this book. I think she even fielded a weepy phone call from me one stressful night when some hag in a production office was mean to me and treated me like an asspill. Jenny said, ". . . I think the biggest reason why you were able to maintain contact was your credibility . . . You're smart and amiable and have a crazy, amazing ability to wrangle people on your end. . . . I think the gist is, you'd propose something, follow through, make it happen and make it happen in the best way possible, all the while respecting our space."

Obviously, Jenny can either not be trusted, or I have her completely fooled into thinking I'm not a total loser, which, of course, I am. There may be something to this syndrome thing. Maybe.

Here's another Anonymous LJ Commenter taking a shot at me

> People have fawned on you for your connections, and I don't think you mind. It gets old. Perceived specialness and actual specialness aren't equal . . . (Anonymous post to Livejournal, February 22, 2006)

Now THAT'S the stuff. Things like this are like smack melting in the spoon. It's soooo bad for me, and ultimately will send me into a funk for days while I try to tiptoe around the internet being as polite and subservient as possible. I don't want anyone to think that I think I'm special. I am the dirt on your shoe, Master Anonymous Commenter, please forgive my transgressions. I completely and unreservedly believe Anonymous that I've been strutting around the internet, namedropping and star-fucking with all of the self-awareness of Paris Hilton. I completely ignore the dozens of posts in my journal that disagree with this. Since I live in constant fear that I'll be discovered to be complete shite, I have to give kudos to those who have the balls to tell me it's so, and dismiss those who disagree.

I was discussing this perplexing situation with my friend Nathan, who just earned a PhD from Caltech in Atomic Physics. I brought up the idea of Imposter Syndrome. He put down his forkful of mashed potatoes and quite seriously said, "I don't have that. I actually *am* incompetent. I've completely fooled everyone into giving me a doctorate. I totally don't deserve it."

I shake my head in disbelief at the newly hooded Doctor Nathan.

"No!" he demands my agreement. "I am truly incompetent. I've never understood it my entire life. My parents would have conferences with my teachers who would gush about how smart I was, and I couldn't believe it. Didn't they know that all these other kids were way smarter? Why couldn't they figure that out?"

Doctor Nathan is off his fucking rocker. He's had a free ride at places like Boston University, Berkeley, and Caltech for years due to his magical genius brain. And he's utterly convinced it has all been a terrible error that could be discovered at any moment. He's nuts, obviously.

I am the one who can't figure out for the life of me why people like me. It seems like a different thing, I know. But to be competent in any sort of event planning activity, I have to gain the trust of people to believe that I'm going to do what I say I'll do. I have to make them like me enough, trust me enough to take my calls, and understand that I'm going to make sure that they look good, that I'll pay the bill, that this will be as simple as possible for them to do what I need to pull off a party or save-our-show campaign. *I* am the rational one, Doctor Nathan is krazy. He's got the Syndrome.

I live my life charging through every project, double checking everything, begging forgiveness on my knees for every typo.

If there's any benefit at all to the terrible Imposter Syndrome, it's that it makes one work harder. Because I'm so desperate to live up to some impossible standard of competency, of honesty, I usually end up doing all right in the world . . . though I do it looking over my shoulder waiting to be caught in a half-truth or a stumble. I'm sure this is what drove Doctor Nathan to the best schools, to working through midnight on experiments and his thesis. The

Syndrome is the thing that pushes me through two a.m. so I can finish an essay and wakes me up four hours later to get to my day job. I think the Syndrome is just that mysterious sort of gravitational pull we call "drive." The mental beatings aren't really so different than the physical beatings one takes in the gym to attain a six pack, or in the ring to beat an opponent and win a pretty sash. It's about the fear of being discovered as lesser, undesirable, incompetent, less than vital.

There's nothing logical about it. The proof of my life is evident in my family's pride in my accomplishments as a fundraiser, a writer, a confidant, the kid who was first in the family to get a Bachelor's degree . . . there's a lot of that. There's more proof of a successful life in the constant circus of dear friends who put aside their lives to help me from drowning in mine. Logic has nothing to do with it.

I have to stay a step ahead of the anonymous zombies running after me who will pounce and point out to everyone what a lying, incompetent fraud I truly am. It's exhausting. And because it's metaphorical running to keep my mind in shape, it doesn't even count toward making my ass smaller.

I fear that if I ever get over The Syndrome, I'll have no motivation at all, and my mind will become stagnant and die a bloated, stinking death. I'll have a nine-hundred pound dead mind that will have to be taken out of my apartment through a window on a crane, and they'll bury it in a piano box.

Because of that great fear, The Syndrome and I will share a symbiotic relationship like a tapeworm and host. I'll feed it all of my neuroses, and it will keep me motivated. I will name my Syndrome "Mabel," and make her my friend. Together, we will someday rule the world, but constantly worry that we're ruling it poorly.

Safe Harbor from Ann Arbor

A stranger I met on the internet came to live with me in April of 2003; a tall, curve-alicious black woman named ita, with a sprinkle of freckles across her nose, close-cropped bleach blond hair, and an ever-present pimp chain draped around her neck. She spells her name with a lower-case "i." She's got a rainbow of belts in a few Martial Arts, a father who was the Jamaican Ambassador for something-or-another, and a mom who's a biochemist. Her accent is decidedly British to mine own ears. When ita enters a room, everyone turns to watch her walk by. She never notices.

She had just crossed two-thousand miles of America, fleeing a stagnant life in Michigan with a sense of ruthless determination to Get the Fuck Out of Dodge. This is a feeling familiar to a lot of the transplanted Americans who packed up their lives on a pilgrimage to Los Angeles in a desperate attempt at hitting the RESET button on their stale lives.

This was the first time I'd ever met ita in person. We never talked much until she came to live with me in my four-hundred-square-foot studio in the Los Feliz neighborhood of L.A.

All I knew about ita I learned from reading her posts on an internet site dedicated to the discussion of a television show called *Buffy the Vampire Slayer*.

The Buffy threads at Salon.com's TableTalk discussion board had become a second cyberhome to me years ago. It was a place where I could spend the hours I wasn't watching television, talking about television. But like any internet community dedicated to any particular subject, conversation eventually evolved into mindless banter, pleas for good karma regarding family and job troubles, political flame wars, and chatter chatter natter natter.

In between posts about marriages teetering on divorce, a racist remark heard on a bus, and socialist views shared by people who were shoved into one too many lockers in high school and have yet to get over it, ita's lament resonated with me.

I had fled the Northeast a year earlier, my soul sucked from my body by a crappy job that had left me nothing but an empty husk. I was marinating in misery until my brain was soft and mushy, falling from my skull like pulled pork. To my great relief, an old friend in L.A. offered me safe harbor so I could get my shit together. ita was in that brain-as-pulled-pork-place and posting her rage at the situation with some regularity. She was packing her bags. She was getting out and punching RESET. My sistah.

I don't think I traded emails or instant messages with ita before she pulled her Michigan Monte Cristo. She didn't know where she would stay, really. She didn't care if she spent her life's savings in a crap hotel in Encino at that point. So I dropped her an email. Told her I'd been there. Someone took me in when I ran, and there was a universal debt to be paid. The Karma Wheel, she had turned, and the arrow was pointed at ita.

And so, she packed her computer, her clothes, and her Palm Pilot into her Volkswagen Jetta, and flipped the town of Satan's Anus, Michigan, the finger. She traveled across the amber waves of grain to California, into the waiting arms of a complete stranger she only knew from a handful of crazy internet posts, who would take her in, keep her fed, and let her start rebuilding her soul.

When she first arrived, we hugged, chatted for an hour, and as she unpacked, I asked, "ita, do you have a last name?"

Four hundred square feet. We were two women way past our college years living in what amounts to a freshman dorm room, and all we knew we had in common was an irrational love of sci-fi television and strangely intimate relationships with People Who Post on the internet. We lived together for three months.

We did alright for two fiercely independent people living in cramped quarters. The closest thing to a battle that we had was the day she put fish soup in the microwave. She taught me how to kickbox. I taught her how to tolerate living with a woefully neurotic chain-smoker. She found a sweet job doing some sort of computer thing at a mortgage company and is saving to buy a house here in California.

She's my family, now. Still, most of our daily conversations take place on the message board she designed while she was recuperating from Michigan on a broken futon on my floor.

On the first anniversary of her move to Los Angeles, ita sent me an email and asked if I would meet her at The House of Pies. I wasn't really aware that it was the anniversary at the time, that she was marking an occasion with something á la mode.

It was a curious thing to me that ita was grateful to me. I always felt a twinge of guilt that I maybe didn't explain to her that my place was so tiny and it'd be more like an inescapable slumber party than a safe haven from Ann Arbor. It wasn't until long after she moved out on her own that I learned ita was deeply sickened by the smell of hard boiled eggs. I live on their cheap, easy protein—like little shelled food-sluts, they are. She never mentioned it, and I still feel awful about gassing her, the poor dear. It's worth mentioning that I could post to her during the day and ask her to take some chicken out of the freezer for supper. My cat, Ruby, offers me no such courtesy in that regard. Nor does Ruby wash the breakfast dishes or bake cookies for me to welcome me home from work. ita was happy to do both of those things. Sometimes I felt like she was hosting me.

I'm not saying I didn't go a little nuts with the constant companionship. I hold my privacy dear, I just hold ita a bit dearer. I knew such would be the case before her dusty Jetta pulled up in front of my apartment building, and I can't sufficiently explain why. It's difficult to express what it is, a certain tone that accompanies the written word perhaps, that forges trust. Absent of body language, what else could it have been that made me so certain that ita would never hurt me, clean out my apartment, and eBay my belongings?

She celebrates her birthday every year by inviting people over to her place and putting out a spread of baked goods and fine tequilas. She never mentions it's her birthday; she doesn't seem to want to mark the day with gifts in her honor. Instead, she spends the day honoring the people who she loves with lemon squares.

Goodness through to the bone. Somewhere, in between the lines of her text, this quality was clear to me, it somehow hummed through the white space. However grateful ita is to me for giving her safe harbor, I return it tenfold for being able to count her as family.

Gay Wedding Tree

In February 2004, San Francisco Mayor Gavin Newsom defied the newly re-elected President Bush's stance on same-sex marriage and started issuing marriage licenses to gay couples in California. Kat and Lori jumped in their car and raced four-hundred miles up to San Francisco to apply for the license and wait in line for six hours to get married in a legal ceremony recognized by the government. They had to hurry before an injunction could stop Newsom's revolution. There was no time for gown fittings and cake tastings and bridesmaids—all the pretty trappings of the traditional ceremony with friends and family rooting for the happy couple.

Bummed about the lack of buttercream frosting and bouquets, Kat started planning a vow-renewal ceremony during the ride back from San Fran, complete with a gift registry, potluck barbecue, and plastic pink flamingo décor. The wedding was to take place in a rented mansion in the mountains, where the thirty-or-so guests were invited to crash for the night after getting plastered on champagne and gorging themselves on barbecued chicken.

My friend Paula and I offered to drive up to the mountains the evening before the wedding to help decorate, cook, and be T-shirt-clad bridesmaids to Kat's self-proclaimed Bridezilla. We arrived around midnight, unpacked the car, and Kat made us grilled cheese sandwiches while Lori put away groceries. We claimed our beds in the rent-a-mansion after inspecting the sheets for anything resembling a semen stain. (It's moments like these that I wish I had one of those *CSI* black lights so I can be totally sure I'm not wrapping myself in a low-thread count evidence bag of indiscretion.) After unsuccessfully trying to find a way to hover a few inches above the pillow, I fell into a mountain-air coma for nine hours.

That morning, Kat handed me two bags of ribbon and asked me to go crazy with the décor. I paced the living room looking for a good place to design an altar with Scotch tape and baby pink curling ribbon.

It was at least a two-smoke job.

I went outside to the front deck to think it over, and that's when I remembered the nasty, cobweb-infested, pre-lit Christmas tree that had been shoved into a dark corner. Brilliant.

"Lori!" I squealed. "Help!"

Lori helped me drag the tree out and center it in the front picture window. We plugged the nasty bastard in, and it surely did light. I ran out to my car and rummaged through the trunk looking for decorations from parties past. I found a box of fifty pink glow sticks, red Mardi Gras beads, and an obscenely large and fuzzy Day-Glo-pink pimp hat. Even more absurd than the items in my trunk was that no one found it weird that they were in there. I rummaged through the bags of decorations Kat and Lori brought with them. Pink flamingo swizzle sticks, yarn, and tea roses.

All of the above were draped on, tucked in, and Scotch-taped to the tree, with the pimp hat dangling atop like a perverse star. The Gay Wedding Tree would greet guests as they arrived, and the guests would instinctively leave wedding gifts under it. It was obnoxiously cheerful, the lesbian love beacon. Somewhere down the mountain there was a Lilac Festival taking place in a small town. Dressing a Christmas tree in drag for a lesbian wedding ceremony during the Lilac

Festival seemed like the right thing to do. It was obviously fate, a lucky day to be married and gay.

Friends started filing through the door in the early afternoon. Robin and Jason arrived to fire up the grill, their gift to the happy couple a cooler full of marinating meat and the stamina to cook outside in May in Southern California sun. ita showed up in a pink gingham dress and white plastic go-go boots, providing fashionista entertainment for all. Kristen's job was to pick up the wrought iron gazebo we had all pitched in to buy for the couple, but she instead showed up with a card and the startling revelation that we were all on crack if we thought a gazebo was going to fit into her Volkswagen Beetle Convertible. Norah and Cody brought their baby daughter Frances and several changes of diapers.

The house filled with chatter and laughter and screams of joy. A chef friend barreled through the door with two gallons of pink buttercream icing and lemon cake. Giggling toddlers twirled in party dresses in between adults peeling vegetables and setting out platters of hummus and pita bread. Babies were passed from hip to hip, while serving spoons full of savory goodness were passed for tasting.

Upstairs the women gathered to help Kat into her gown and fix her hair. Lori changed into an Armani tux while Kat fussed with a veil. The happy-busy din of wedding guests slipped in and out of the cracks under the doors and suddenly it was time for the ceremony.

We all ran downstairs to the living room where a friend waited, Palm Pilot full of vows in hand. She had been ordained in the Universal Life Church Monastery, which is a free online ordaining service for those who may want to officiate a wedding at some point in their lives. Lori stood at the landing of the stairs waiting for Kat to hustle out of one of the guest rooms. The music started and Kat marched. Kristen chased after her with the bouquet she forgot on the bathroom counter.

We gathered huddled on couches, cross-legged on the floor, bunched together, faces masked with digital cameras. I think Jason still had a spatula in his hand from the grill. The ceremony only lasted a few minutes, a short reaffirmation of vows taken up north three months earlier.

". . . and I now pronounce you spouses for life."

Kat and Lori reached out and held onto each other while flashes popped and the guests cheered.

We all got drunk and licked pink icing from chocolate cupcakes. We passed champagne around, drinking deep straight from the bottle and gossiping most recklessly. Lori's engineer colleagues presented the happy couple with an enormous, curiously lightweight cardboard box. A thousand origami cranes poured out onto the floor, honoring the Japanese tradition that if one is blessed with a thousand cranes, one will lead a fortunate and long life. The engineers dared us to count. We were way too drunk for math and took them at their word. The engineers seemed a little let down that we didn't rise to the challenge.

I passed out early, as I am the World's Cheapest Date, and woke up to a breakfast of omelets and fresh coffee served by the again newlyweds to the small handful of us who stayed for cleanup duty. We all curled up on the couches in our pajamas and played with Norah and Cody's daughter (who managed to fit inside a teakettle gift box) while opening wedding gifts, and then settled in to watch DVDs and graze on leftover wedding cake.

It didn't occur to me until much later, but I met all these people on the internet, and most of these people met each other on the internet. I always assume if I don't know someone, it's because they don't have access to the internet. Even Kat and Lori met each other on an internet fanlisting for folk/alt/country/rock singer Ani DiFranco. Nothing about this seems weird to me, but I often wonder if my mom would worry if she knew my method of friend-finding.

On the way home from the festivities, Paula remarked that she felt like a bridesmaid. She had never been one before. I relayed that to Kat in some passing instant message conversation weeks later.

She said, "You *were* bridesmaids. You're family."

I agreed.

Random Acts of PayPal

If you listen to my family or the evening news, the internet is a haven for ax murderers and rapists, waiting to lure you out of your house to steal your identity, gut you, eat your spleen, and mail your head to the local authorities. At the very least, everyone on the net is either a drooling fiend luring young suburban girls into sexual slavery, or some slimy snake-oil salesman who can drain your checking account just by learning your email address.

My family tends to use the net solely to send me ASS-CAPS EMAILS WARNING ME ABOUT WOMEN BEING ACCOSTED IN PARKING LOTS BY SEXUAL PREDATORS or FWD: CHAIN-EMAILS ABOUT BILL

GATES SENDING A MILLION DOLLARS FOR FORWARDING THIS EMAIL TO ONE HUNDRED PEOPLE. I gently explain to my family that this is how viruses spread, and then link them to the Snopes.com, an urban legend reference website so they can see that these are in fact urban legends, and that Bill Gates has no way to track forwards. If he did, it'd mean he could peer into your inbox, and isn't that sort of creepy? It doesn't actually help, they relentlessly send me this crap anyway, and think I'm an asshole for spoiling their fun.

When my friend Susan, a writer for the infamously hilarious TelevisionWithoutPity.com website, first told her mom that she was hired to write recaps online, her mom responded by telling her to never give "them" her Social Security number. "My mom thought it was a scam," she explained. Susan's mom, like my mom, is suspicious of all things net related.

I've never had anything stolen from me by strangers on the Net. Nor has anyone snuck into my window and raped my cat in the middle of the night. My experiences with strangers on the net have mostly chiseled away at my cynic's soul. Over the past five or six years I've been comforted with care packages filled with tea and bath salts, the occasional bouquet of flowers, gift certificates to spas, and once I even got a DVD player for no apparent reason from a gorgeous woman who had a rebate for one, saw me post something about not being able to splurge on a player, and generously sent me my beloved JVC. I never asked for these things, and none of these people asked for anything in return. I don't know that these things are deserved, but maybe it's karma in action, if such a thing exists.

I've orchestrated many random acts of PayPal myself. PayPal.com is a website that allows anyone to send money to anyone else, using their credit card or bank account. Occasionally, the internet communities in which I live will be inspired to give a collective gift to charity or to a deserving individual, and I've opened my PayPal account for donations so I could write the check or buy the gift on behalf of everyone. I always provide an accounting and post the thank you notes, so people feel comfortable and secure sending me cash.

My favorite random act of PayPal resulted in a plane ticket, a visa, and a five-city tour of the United States for one stranger on the Net, a wee Israeli woman named Nilly. Nilly practiced her English by reading and responding to the posts at Salon.com's TableTalk message boards.

Nilly is beloved by all of us Buffistas, the group of a hundred or so netizens who gathered at TableTalk to discuss *Buffy* and *Angel,* and natter on about the uses of duct tape and salad shooters. Nilly is a Physics grad student, and despite growing up in a war zone, or perhaps because of it, has an overwhelming passion for life that leaves everyone who reads her posts intoxicated with gratitude for simply having woken up that morning. In between bombings and *Buffy,* Nilly would carefully compose posts, toggling between a Hebrew-to-English dictionary, occasionally asking for clarification on grammar. She's one of those souls who never takes part in quarrels, and can stop a ridiculously acidic argument cold just by posting a simple "hello."

It's not a guilt thing; it's just that her sheer presence on the planet assures one that even a cubic ton of bullshit is a tiny thing in comparison to getting on a bus to go to work every morning that could explode due to some deluded fanatic with a pound of plastique taped to his ignorant ass. And there's Nilly, genuine in her cheerfulness, content in her skin, her head full of plans for the future. How can one not feel the vibration of hopefulness emanating from the computer screen?

So, yes, everyone loves Nilly. From time to time, Nilly would dreamily post a desire to meet all of the people she'd been reading all these years. And we all wished there wasn't such a huge distance between us, so we could actually sit over tea and hear her voice express all of that hopefulness we'd been drinking in on the net for so long.

One afternoon, my friend Kristen and I were sitting on our asses watching television, and Kristen said, "Wouldn't it be cool if we raised enough money to buy Nilly a ticket to L.A.?"

It would have seemed a passive question, if you didn't know either Kristen or me, but the truth of the matter is that between the two of us, we've seen about $50,000 pass through our PayPal accounts for acts more random than this. Flowers to cheer or congratulate, a pile of books to welcome a new baby, divvying up a Christmas wish list of toys to be purchased for the children of a family falling on hard times, these things occur organically on message boards all the time. Collecting enough to bring a friend from the Middle East to the States was an enormous undertaking. We're either arrogant or foolish enough to think any idea worth verbalizing is a good idea and so rarely mention anything we think is impossible.

We didn't discuss it further, and continued sitting on our asses watching the TV. But a couple weeks later, late at night, another Buffista pondered the idea online. I mentioned that we could in fact raise that sort of money, if we put our collective finances together. We posed the question to Nilly, who was initially afraid to take us up on the offer, feeling undeserving, maybe. Eventually, she caved and accepted the gift of the ticket. Our friend Tim Minear, the richest of us all due to a lucrative contract to produce television for 20th Century Fox, piped up with an offer that he'd pay half if we raised the other half. One minute later, he PayPaled me a cool grand.

The following are the posts from the night at Buffistas.org that lead to the greatest random act of PayPal I've ever seen unfold (all grammatical errors belong to respective posters):

NoiseDesign - Mar 14, 2004, 12:05:00 a.m. PST, #4576 of 10012

We really need to arrange for Nilly to get here someday. How hard is travel to the U.S. from Israel?

Trudy Booth - Mar 14, 2004, 12:08:14 a.m. PST, #4577 of 10012

I think the problem is that Nilly is a starving student living on kosher ramen.

Allyson - Mar 14, 2004, 12:08:24 a.m. PST, #4578 of 10012

Damnit.

"How hard is travel to the U.S. from Israel?"

Oh just visiting? A very long flight, customs, a ticket (2 grand, prolly), and then we'd all take turns feeding our Nilly and putting her up for the night.

Kristen suggested we take up a collection. I'm in.

Tim Minear - Mar 14, 2004, 12:10:09 a.m. PST, #4582 of 10012

"Kristen suggested we take up a collection. I'm in."

If Buffistas raise half, I'll pony up the other half to get her here.

Nilly - Mar 14, 2004, 12:10:45 a.m. PST, #4583 of 10012

It's not hard - it does demand getting a visa (around a couple of months of waiting for that once one's gone over all the bureaucratic procedures), and a little bit more money than I can afford right now. Oh, and for me I'd prefer it to be not on the middle of the semester when I have TAing duties that I've already committed to.

Right now I'd say the real problem in the timing.

KristinT - Mar 14, 2004, 12:12:25 a.m. PST, #4588 of 10012

I'm new, but I'm all for the "helping people travel" thing. Plus, that's an incredibly generous offer Tim made. I'm impressed.

I'm in. Give me a place to send my money. Other than on April 15th. Unfortunately, in terms of sending money places, that day's taken.

We have to file in 37 states. Feel sorry for me.

Allyson - Mar 14, 2004, 12:13:09 a.m. PST, #4589 of 10012

"If Buffistas raise half, I'll pony up the other half to get her here."

I marked it. You're on.

Tim Minear - Mar 14, 2004 12:14:03 am PST #4590 of 10012

" I marked it. You're on."

Cool.

NoiseDesign - Mar 14, 2004, 12:16:31 a.m. PST, #4595 of 10012

"If Buffistas raise half, I'll pony up the other half to get her here."

I'm in for at least $100.

Nilly - Mar 14, 2004 12:17:09 am PST #4597 of 10012

Notice how I try to ignore you guys being crazy generous, because I can't believe strangers-on-the-internet are being so amazing. It needs some time to sink in.

Allyson - Mar 14, 2004, 12:17:54 a.m. PST, #4600 of 10012

Damnit.

YOU ALL BETTER NOT BE KIDDING BECAUSE I'LL OPEN
MY PAYPAL ACCOUNT IN THE MORNING.

KristinT - Mar 14, 2004, 12:18:16 a.m. PST, #4601 of 10012

Someone should set up a PayPal account to collect. I'm in
for $50.

Nilly - Mar 14, 2004 12:18:38 am PST #4602 of 10012

ALLYSON!

Allyson - Mar 14, 2004, 12:21:42 a.m. PST, #4610 of 10012

I have a Paypal account. We use it for charitable and
goodly works here, all the time.

---

billytea - Mar 14, 2004 12:22:12 am PST #4611 of 10012

I'll happily contribute to getting Nilly over here for the [face to face meeting].

Tim Minear - Mar 14, 2004, 12:22:55 a.m. PST, #4613 of 10012

This is just like the end of "It's A Wonderful Life!" Only in color! It is in color, yeah?

Jon B. - Mar 14, 2004, 12:23:36 a.m. PST, #4615 of 10012

You can count me in, too.

NoiseDesign - Mar 14, 2004, 12:25:28 a.m. PST, #4619 of 10012

Perkins just relayed through IM that she's in for $100 as well. And she says Hi to Nilly.

Nilly - Mar 14, 2004, 12:25:34 a.m. PST, #4620 of 10012

" This is just like the end of "It's A Wonderful Life!" Only in color!"

It definitely feels like a movie. As in, not real.

Cass - Mar 14, 2004, 12:26:49 a.m. PST, #4623 of 10012

(really perkins, visiting Cass) I'm in for 100 as well. If Nilly visiting LA is in the picture, she can stay with me while here.

Tim Minear - Mar 14, 2004, 12:28:31 a.m. PST, #4626 of 10012

Bad timing for Nilly right this second. She gets to choose the time with her school and all. The money will only ripen.

Allyson - Mar 14, 2004, 12:30:00 a.m. PST, #4627 of 10012

"Nilly's coming to LA for sure, though, right?"

Waiting for Nilly to peel herself off the ceiling to let us know.

What say you, Nilly?

All you have to do is pack a bag, and we got your back.

Jon B. - Mar 14, 2004, 12:30:56 a.m. PST, #4628 of 10012

Fares from Tel Aviv to LA are in the neighborhood of $1000, not $2000. This should be easier than rescuing George Bailey.

NoiseDesign - Mar 14, 2004, 12:31:23 a.m. PST, #4629 of 10012

If they are that price I think we've already got the cost of the ticket raised.

Nilly - Mar 14, 2004, 12:31:26 a.m. PST, #4630 of 10012

The semester ends on the end of June, I think. But in the summer the flights and everything is much more expensive because everybody takes vacations then. The next semester doesn't start until the end of October, though. So maybe sometime before that.

You have no idea how tempting this is. No idea.

KristinT - Mar 14, 2004, 12:32:07 a.m. PST, #4632 of 10012

Really going to bed now. I hate to even ask this, but how many posts are likely to accumulate in this thread between now and tomorrow? Will I be able to *find* the PayPal account? :-)

I'm so happy that Good Things are happening my first day hanging around here.

Holli - Mar 14, 2004, 12:32:29 a.m. PST, #4634 of 10012

I'm a college student. So I can probably afford $10-20.

I'd only spend it on comic books and Easy Mac.

Nilly - Mar 14, 2004,12:36:34 a.m. PST, #4642 of 10012

I'm really embarrassed by this - it's not that I can't afford the trip myself, with some arranging and tightening-the-belt and stuff. I don't really need the help.

Not bad embarrassed! Overwhelmed by the generosity and the kindness and the wonderfulness embarrassed! I'm nearly in tears!

Allyson - Mar 14, 2004, 12:38:38 a.m. PST, #4646 of 10012

Do I hear a yes from Nilly? C'mon. You're depriving me of sleep. Let us bring you here.

NoiseDesign - Mar 14, 2004, 12:38:52 a.m. PST, #4647 of 10012

"I don't really need the help."

Nilly, for me at least, it's about me wanting to do it. Money gets spent in all kinds of lame ways all the time, and, well, this is a way that is anything but lame.

Tim Minear - Mar 14, 2004, 12:39:04 a.m. PST, #4649 of 10012

"it's not that I can't afford the trip myself, with some arranging and tightening-the-belt and stuff."

Yeah, but why? Also, we all know you'd just keep being all pragmatic and putting it off. So go fer it.

Nilly - Mar 14, 2004, 12:41:06 a.m. PST, #4650 of 10012

Sorry - I had to answer the phone and it was a sick friend, and I needed to help her arrange stuff and pretend I'm not [excited].

I honestly don't know what to say. I'm completely overwhelmed.

P.M. Marcontell - Mar 14, 2004, 12:41:07 a.m. PST, #4651 of 10012

I'm in for Nillying Nilly.

Trudy Booth - Mar 14, 2004, 12:43:00 a.m. PST, #4653 of 10012

My unemployed-ass can't chip in as of now, but you get to NY the offer to put you up and get you fed still stands.

Allyson - Mar 14, 2004, 12:45:03 a.m. PST, #4656 of 10012

Standing by, Nilly.

Okay. In case I go to bed while Nilly goes through all this [excitement], my Paypal is at [redacted].

If Nilly gets all ridiculous and turns us down, I'll just send the money back.

My birthday is this month, Nilly. For my birthday, i want you to say yes and come visit us. So there. Now you have opposing guilt. HA!

Allyson - Mar 14, 2004, 12:50:29 a.m. PST, #4667 of 10012

Dear God, I need sleep, but I'm all excited and stuff!

Nilly - Mar 14, 2004, 12:51:47 a.m. PST, #4670 of 10012

OK, I'm back.

There's something that Hec once told me. About presents. That the beautiful thing about a gift is that it isn't earned or paid for. It only goes out one way into the world. And if one wants to honor the gift, then they accept it graciously, and give their own gifts out into the world. When they have an abundance to share.

So it's not like your amazing generosity has anything to do about *me*. It's about you, and therefore, if I want to honor *you*, I'm going to accept it. And not return it - just give back when I can.

Goodness, I guess it just means I've said yes.

Edit: I'm in tears right now, for the record. You have no idea how touched I am.

Allyson - Mar 14, 2004, 12:56:33 a.m. PST, #4676 of 10012

[email redacted]

That's my paypal addie. Send in donations for Nilly's airfare.

Nilly, you should email me at that addie when you have an idea of when you can come so I can buy your ticket.

Let me know if you need help with the tourist visa.

Tim Minear - Mar 14, 2004, 12:58:01 a.m. PST, #4679 of 10012

Perfect example of when "nice" is so much better than "funny."

Sent you a grand, Allyson.

Allyson - Mar 14, 2004, 1:01:09 a.m. PST, #4681 of 10012

Tim. I so mean this in every way possible. I love you.

Tim Minear - Mar 14, 2004, 1:03:51 a.m. PST, #4684 of 10012

Oh, go to bed, Allyson.

Astarte - Mar 14, 2004, 1:06:23 a.m. PST, #4686 of 10012

YAY!!!!!! Nilly's coming to US!!!

I'm in for $50.

Nilly - Mar 14, 2004 1:07:08 a.m. PST, #4688 of 10012

Around 95% of the visa requests are approved, as far as I can tell (yeah, I've checked). They don't approve people who are suspected in arriving for unauthorized work or for crimes. I'm a student, so I think it's going to be OK.

It takes about 2 months to get an answer about a visa. The semester ends on the end of June (yeah, I've checked that, too). Then there are the exams, so the summer will probably begin in earnest at the end of July or the beginning of August. And the holidays start at the middle of September, so I have some time until then.

This could really work.

Allyson? Whenever you think something less-than-wonderful about yourself, please let me know. I think you're absolutely one-of-a-kind, in the best possible way.

And, Tim? I - no, I'm not sure I really know what to say. I've loved your writing for some time now, from long before I saw your posts here, but now seeing your name on a TV screen will have so much more meaning. *Thank you.*

Allyson - Mar 14, 2004, 1:14:33 a.m. PST, #4692 of 10012

"I think you're absolutely one-of-a-kind, in the best possible way."

Twas Kristen's idea. I was just the loon that was awake.

Tim Minear - Mar 14, 2004, 1:17:57 a.m. PST, #4695 of 10012

Nilly, you're welcome.

Allyson - Mar 14, 2004, 1:20:49 a.m. PST, #4696 of 10012

"I'm going to bed, now."

No, seriously. C'mon! It was all exciting and stuff!

So. Love Tim. Love Kristen. Love Nilly.

Nilly, don't forget to email me your details and such so we can coordinate the getting of your ticket and such.

I'd suggest getting a refundable ticket while you work on your visa, so we can get a better price, now.

RobertH - Mar 14, 2004, 1:30:54 a.m. PST, #4700 of 10012

. . . did that just happen?

I'm up way too late, and I'm checking back in one more time, and HOLY SHIT there's almost 200 new posts in the middle of the night. And you absolutely deserve all of that, Nilly. I'm too tired right now, but I'll try to chip in a bit tomorrow.

(Assuming the thing isn't all paid for already by then. And to think, Jerry Lewis goes to all that trouble of calling Carrot Top every year.)

Tim . . . you're a good man. Too bad about getting fired from *BtVS*.

. . . did that just happen?

Nilly - Mar 14, 2004, 1:31:36 a.m. PST, #4701 of 10012

I'm going to save all these messages and read over them again and again, just to make sure they are really real and not some fantasy that's only in my head.

You guys have no idea.

I couldn't ever dream, in my wildest imaginations, anything like this. Neither of you has ever met me, and still you're being so generous, and so kind regarding this generosity. I think I'm so rich by meeting you, and I definitely do *not* mean the money.

Allyson, I'll e you when you're more awake, OK?

---

aurelia - Mar 14, 2004, 1:36:50 a.m. PST, #4703 of 10012

Damn. A thread has never made me teary before. And I thought I was going to go to bed at a decent hour.

If we raise enough can we have a Nilly North American Tour 2004 (t-shirts and all)? I can provide a bed in Chicago.

P.M. Marcontell - Mar 14, 2004, 1:46:59 a.m. PST, #4704 of 10012

"Before you read this, allow me to explain the difference between Elongated Man and Plastic Man." - Seth Cohen (property of Kat)

Nilly, even if I don't get to see you, I'm thoroughly thrilled at the very notion of it even being possible, as you always make me smile.

Nilly - Mar 14, 2004, 1:54:03 a.m. PST, #4705 of 10012

I still don't believe this is for real. You know the scene in "A Little Princess" when the Indian Gentleman secretly puts beautiful things in her room, and she had had a horrible day and then her hopes were raised by her friend's package, and then the headmistress crashed them and she woke up to the magical completely surprising wonderfulness and she touched a hot coal, on purpose, to make sure it was real and not just a dream of hers?

Well, I'm nothing near anything like the situation of that character in the book. But I'm staring at the posts and trying to make myself believe this is really a reality and not just a fantasy or a scene from a story I tell myself. You people are just too much. And I hope I'll get to say it to each and every one of you *personally*.

Nope, still doesn't feel real.

I have to walk away from the computer for a while - I wonder if all those posts will still be here when I get back, and will still have the same meaning when I re-read them then.

---

ita - Mar 14, 2004, 5:48:06 a.m. PST, #4709 of 10012

NILLY!

I'm so glad I moved to LA. So when Kristen gets ideas, and Allyson gets bossy, and Tim gets . . . god Tim, you're marvelous . . . I'll be able to take Nilly to krav!

Hil R. - Mar 14, 2004, 8:29:39 a.m. PST, #4721 of 10012

Wow. Once again, totally amazed at the Buffistas, and Tim.

I've only got a few dollars to contribute, but Nilly, if you ever end up in DC and was a non-motel-y place to crash, the offer to stay at my place still stands.

———————————————————————

Allyson - Mar 14, 2004, 9:42:11 a.m. PST, #4728 of 10012

I don't know that this is Pressworthy, but I'm just so honored to know all of you. We're about $300 shy of matching Tim's grand. I think we should be able to get Nilly something in business class (because an international flight from Israel? blows in coach).

Truly am honored to have a really teensy part in making this happen. Someone in another thread said Nilly is the heart of the board, and that's true.

Your generosity sparkles and dances. When fit hits the shan around here, remember this. This sort of connection with the world is what the net is for.

Well, and porn.

Now we just need to get in a hella fight about who gets Nilly and for how long, which is a nice fight to have.

We're definitely bringing her here.

Thank you.

Kristen - Mar 14, 2004, 10:17:26 a.m. PST, #4740 of 10012

Sheesh. I go to bed early and I miss a party.

But Nilly's coming to town! This is so cool. Allyson rocks. Tim's a sweetie. The rest of you are pretty freaking fabulous as well.

ETA: Oh and there's a new Kristin-shaped person. Hello new Kristin-shaped person!

Steph L. - Mar 14, 2004, 10:23:44 a.m. PST, #4745 of 10012

Wow. I just have no words. Buffistas' generosity has, yet again, outdone itself.
Everyone who says that internet communities aren't *real* community can just bite me.

Tim, you are a good, good man.

Sophie Max - Mar 14, 2004, 10:54:25 a.m. PST, #4778 of 10012

peeking in

Allyson . . . will you accept paypal in Canadian dollars? I didn't think to change it to US dollars, and then got the little warning sign. DOH.

signed, a lurker trying to support Nilly in email, but not being very good at it.

Allyson - Mar 14, 2004 10:58:45 am PST #4786 of 10012

"Allyson . . . will you accept paypal in Canadian dollars?"

Your money is suspect. It comes in funny colors and smells like Canada.

Paypal converts it. It's all good.

Narrator - Mar 14, 2004, 11:14:37 a.m. PST, #4796 of 10012

Hey, I'm gone for a few hours and you folks are flying Nilly across several time zones and such. Whee. Allyson, you'll get some $$ from me for the "Nilly and Buffistas Excellent Adventure." But it's coming snail mail because newfangled things confuzzle me.

UTTAD - Mar 14, 2004, 11:27:23 a.m. PST, #4810 of 10012

Just read about Nilly. Cool, beyond words cool.

Um, can I get a bike?

In three days, we raised $3,000. A record. Nilly was stunned, and a little scared about how she would explain this to her family, who like my family, would automatically assume we would either sell Nilly into sexual slavery or make a fine kosher sausage out of her.

It was spring, and Nilly would be able to take some vacation time in the summer. So for the next few months we planned her itinerary: Tel Aviv to Los Angeles, Los Angeles to San Francisco, San Francisco to Boston, Boston to New

York, New York to D.C., and back to New York for a flight from JFK back to Israel over a three-week period. We got her a visa, her traveler's health insurance, and had some walking-around money to spare. I corresponded with Nilly, helping her with the visa application and insurance. Meanwhile, all the Buffistas who were going to house and feed Nilly during her stay had a crash course in kosher rules and regulations, as our girl is an Orthodox Jew. Her San Francisco host, Deb, prepared to blowtorch her oven in anticipation of Nilly's arrival.

Me, I just figured we'd wing it and picked up some kosher soup and a new pot, and unscrewed the light bulb in the fridge so Nilly could get a drink of water in the middle of the night during the Sabbath without worrying about turning on a light.

The day Nilly landed at LAX was coated in a sugary glaze of the surreal. I wandered around the Bradley International Terminal, convinced that my being the usual twenty minutes late caused Nilly to get back on the plane to Tel Aviv. I couldn't find her anywhere, and really, I'd never even actually seen her, so I didn't even know who I was looking for. I wandered back outside, feeling like a loser for not making a bigger, more colorful sign reading, "NILLY." As I turned back toward the terminal, there was a two-hundred-foot Star of David reflected in the glass from the tail of an El Al airplane. It was as if God himself was sending me a sign: "Nilly is in this building, Jackass!"

So I ran back into the terminal, and moments later, a tiny young woman with olive skin and long, black, shiny hair was running toward me laughing my name and throwing her arms around me. Our Nilly girl in the flesh was like that second when the kernel of corn explodes inside out in a pan of hot oil. You expect it to happen, but still it's a delightful surprise that makes you blink despite yourself.

We never stopped talking the whole way back to my place, and Nilly was fascinated by West Hollywood, where a good portion of the storefront signage is written in Hebrew. I told her that Tim, the biggest benefactor of this trip was taking us out to dinner at a kosher restaurant later that evening. Tim is Nilly's favorite screenwriter, and for the first time since she crashed into me in the terminal, she was quiet. She watched the WeHo world go by outside the car window, lost in a new environment. I was left thinking maybe she didn't understand the English. Fans crowd Tim at conventions, seeking autographs and a moment of his attention. Not only did Tim pony up a hefty amount of cash for Nilly's visit, but he was also setting aside an ample amount of time to buy her dinner. It eventually sank in and she smiled so widely I thought it might swallow her whole face. When we got to my apartment, she handed me a small package, a pot with soil and seeds from Israel, a tiny piece of earth from the Middle East. There was also a home warming prayer etched in silver, molded in the shape of a hand, with the translation carefully typed in English.

We had a small adventure shopping for kosher groceries in Los Angeles, Nilly pausing in front of an SUV parked in the garage to wonder why anyone would need a tank in the suburbs of a country not fighting off suicide bombers. "Everything is SO BIG here!" Nilly burst. I was secretly ashamed. I'm in love with much of America, but the SUV thing makes me irrationally angry. I think I'd be cool with it if most people actually, you know, went camping in them, but mostly they're just bullshit pieces of bling.

Nilly stayed with me for a few days before Lee picked her up to tour Hollywood, and then drove her up the coast to San Francisco with Drew, where she stayed with Deb, who took her to the airport where she met up with the Boston crew. She was then on her way to New York to stay with Rebecca and then Leah, respectively, and then to Hil in D.C.

At each place, she was welcomed by these strangers on the net, who took time off from work and planned sightseeing tours of their home cities. They provided phone numbers and emergency contact info should Nilly's family worry that the stereotype of the bloodthirsty internet maniac might bear out on their beloved daughter. I'm not entirely sure if Nilly ever fully explained to her parents how she came to be in possession of that plane ticket. "Mom, Dad, a bunch of people on a message board and a Hollywood producer put together a ton of cash to buy me a tour of America. No, I'm sure it's safe." Hm. I wouldn't tell my parents the truth, either. Like my friend Susan's mom, I'm sure Nilly's parents would think it was a scam and tie her to a chair until she turned forty. Nilly explained that the year before, she'd received an invitation to a wedding from a couple of Buffistas in San Francisco who met and fell in love on the message board; the invitation came with a note that explained that if she should be able to make it to the U.S., they would of course provide a kosher meal. Nilly's mother softened about us, the internet strangers, because of that small note of consideration of Nilly's religious beliefs.

To Nilly, none of us were strangers. She told me that we all looked exactly how she imagined us. (I wish she had imagined I was thinner and taller.) She said she kept trying to remind herself that personalities she knew only from the internet might not mirror who they actually are in "real life." It turned out that everyone she met on Nilly's North American Tour matched up with the images in her head, only more vibrant and three-dimensional. One night, a few friends popped over to my apartment for a visit, and Nilly fell asleep while we talked late into the night, curled up in a corner, safe and content.

Nilly's stay in the U.S. seemed frighteningly short. One second we were buying traveler's checks, the next, someone posted that Nilly was safely delivered to JFK where she would be taking a long flight back to the Middle East.

I was terribly sad that it was over, that I would probably never see my friend Nilly again, for the rest of my life. Have you ever said goodbye to someone you genuinely love, knowing that you would live out the rest of your lives never seeing each other ever again? I didn't really think about that when Nilly left my apartment. As long as she was on U.S. soil, I could hop on a red-eye and see her in five hours at the most. Shit, I could take a long nap in the air and wake up and have breakfast with her, that same day.

So when I read the board, and saw that she would be leaving, I felt like I was sinking in tar, a little helpless. I wanted to call JFK and say, "Wait, I want to spend another day with you in our pajamas eating hummus 'til noon, talking about traffic jams on the Gaza strip."

That's when my phone rang, and it was Nilly, from the international terminal at JFK. She called to tell me that New

York was the most alive place she'd ever seen, that even the sidewalks seemed to breathe, then you realize it's the subway moving under your feet. She said thank you, thank you, thank you, a dozen times. She said she wouldn't forget this, ever. Every syllable was punctuated with gratitude and a promise that she would come back, someday. That we'd sit and talk for hours. Her English had progressed so quickly over the few weeks she was here that I had to ask her to slow down. My stomach ached and my eyes welled up, because though I know she was genuine to the bone about her promise to come back again, life has a way of getting sticky and full, and promises don't so much get broken . . . sometimes, they just tend to fade with the wear of the calendar pages flipping.

I hope to see my dear friend again, someday.

Together, Alone

I absolutely, completely, unconditionally love my family. I do. Living three-thousand miles from them makes me appreciate them all the more. Especially during the holidays.

If I don't have to spend Thanksgiving with my family, I can retain fond memories of them and not be reminded that they are sort of like a Woody Allen film on crank, and with irritable bowel syndrome. Holidays usually end up a screech-fest of anger that would be better off repressed. I start to twitch in a Pavlovian manner when I smell turkey, acutely aware that an insane argument will break out at any moment after a couple of passive-aggressive barbs jabbed viciously at the gut of the slowest running Beatrice in the pack.

But I love them. They're my family. I swear, I really love them. I would just rather see them individually, since once amassed over the carcass of a twelve pound bird, they can't help but go Hiroshima at the table.

I can easily avoid this now by going home after Christmas, claiming poverty or crappy airline ticket availability. This allows me to see the family in drips and drabs, in a calm environment. It also means I mostly get my nephew to myself, so we can make up games and race in a go-cart over my mom's hardwood floors while pumping our fists in the air and yelling, "WE DON'T NEED NO STINKIN' BUGGIES!" No, I don't know what it means, either. He's two. Give the kid a break.

This means I'm usually alone for the holidays, unless some of my other friends who don't have family here in L.A. decide to meet up at Mel's and have a hot-turkey sandwich on a weirdly deserted Sunset Strip.

This past fall, my friend Kat instant messaged me with a proposal. A group of us internet fandom junkies were going to rent a beach house on Catalina Island, off the coast of Long Beach. We'd have Thanksgiving with each other, the family we had cobbled together through the magic of the World Wide Web. I was assigned to bring mashed potatoes, as that is the only dish I can cook. It was to be me, Kat 'n'

Lori (from the Gay Wedding Tree), ita (whom I gave safe harbor from Ann Arbor), Kristen (we tried to save *Firefly* together), Lee, Sara, and Paula.

Paula doesn't have her own story in this collection, which is odd, since she's one of the cornerstones of my life. She was one of the first message board people I ever met "in real life." We both were working in Boston at the time, and we both grew up with moms who waited tables at Route 1 restaurants North of Boston. Meeting each other after so much online chatting was a natural progression, and I liked her immediately. She moved to Los Angeles a few months before I did, and became a de facto sister. I sat in a dentist's office for hours while she got her wisdom teeth pulled under several shots of Novocain, and she scooped me up off the curb at LAX the night it took me twelve hours, a death-defying cab ride from Newark Airport to JFK, and two planes to get back to L.A. from the East Coast . . . and my luggage was lost. Forever. We're each other's emergency contacts on all the work and insurance forms, so if either of us is ever crushed by a falling cubicle wall, HR will let me or her know so we can make arrangements for sending the body back to Boston. Or something like that.

Paula is a self-proclaimed doormat. It's so easy to walk all over her, one has to be careful where one steps to avoid mashing a heel into her nose. This all changes when Paula is in the passenger side of a car, though. She starts barking orders about rights and lefts. She tells me when a light is turning red three blocks away. I always ask, "Paula, how do you think I drive to work every day without you there to direct me?" And she'll respond by barking more orders. I often think that if Paula would like to stop being a doormat, she should drag a front car seat with her on a wagon wherever she goes. She could be making a six figure salary by now if she employed such an idea when negotiating her raise every year.

Paula was in the backseat when we drove to Long Beach to catch the ferry to Catalina Island, making the ride less like a military exercise. Kristen rode shotgun, my Sister Smoker, in order to share the ashtray.

Two hours later we were dragging our luggage onto the dock, and Lori was there to meet us, driving a small golf cart. She gave us a brief tour of the island. Not brief because she was in a hurry, but brief because the island is half the size of Providence, Rhode Island. Everything in Catalina is bizarrely small. The ambulances are slightly bigger golf carts tricked out with sirens. White picket fences were no higher than my knees, and I'm four foot ten.

Our weekend rental was big enough for the eight of us to sleep comfortably; three bedrooms, a pull-out couch, and a regular couch in the living room. Lee and Paula volunteered to sleep in the living room, since both were under the death grip of nasty colds, and were producing infected snot at an alarming rate of fifty Kleenex per hour.

Parked in front of the fireplace, draped in a winter coat and huddled under a blanket, ita quietly read a book, looking like a Hip Hop version of Whistler's Mother. Despite spending several winters in Montreal, Michigan, and the UK, ita has never lost her Jamaican internal temperature control and sleeps in heavy socks in L.A. in June.

The first night at the rental was the beginning of a bizarre ritual. I changed into pajamas, washed my face, and brushed my teeth. That's not part of the bizarre ritual. The bizarre thing was how quiet it was when I emerged from the bathroom at nine p.m. rounded the corner into the living room, and everyone save Paula and me were silently curled up on the couches with their laptops open. Free wireless internet was an unadvertised amenity, apparently. I laughed. Paula grabbed a camera and took some shots of everyone bathed in the cool glow of the Web. And then we all passed out before ten p.m.

Early to bed, early to rise and so I found myself shuffling to the bathroom at six a.m. the following morning. In the dining room, around the table, sipping tea, were Sara, and Lori, looking a little alien with their faces underlit by computer screens. It bothered me. I don't have a laptop and was insanely jealous of my housemates cheerily reading celebrity gossip and I thought maybe we were all insane.

Kat, in her usual breezy and matter-of-fact way explained that we were a house full of introverts—except for Paula, who's an obvious extrovert. It doesn't have anything to do with being strong-willed or shy. It's all about what saps your energy. For introverts, being engaged with lots of other people drains the brain, and at the end of the day, we recharge with solitude. For an extrovert, solitude is an energy-suck, and so people like Paula head out to Sonny McLean's for a drink and the Red Sox game after work, to recharge by being surrounded by boisterous people.

We all met through the internet, on message boards discussing television shows. Both things are such solitary activities. Watching television is a voyeuristic connection to people who can't respond to you. It's sort of like watching the monkeys at the zoo, without the primates on the other side of the glass pitching dung at the viewer . . . unless one is watching FOX, the dung network. There's still the barrier of a glass screen when posting on the internet. But the dung flinging is interactive.

From the introvert perspective, there's peacefulness to being able to engage with hundreds of people while absorbing the quiet Zen of being alone. From an extrovert's perspective, it's the engagement with people, relieving the feeling of being alone. Our vacation destination makes sense when you consider that we were a house full of introverts. We chose to stay on a small island off the coast of Long Beach in the off-season, when the fewest tourists would be visiting.

While providing sounding board service to one of my many bosses in the tangled matrix of line-management at my day job, I found myself suffering an earnest need to defend the merits of the internet as a valuable communication tool. He was worried about the effects of the net on his daughter, who was absorbed in instant messaging software, chat rooms, and MySpace.com. His argument was that electronic communication, with its constant multitasking between screens filled with people screaming hyperbole into the ether was turning interpersonal engagement into high speed shorthand, devoid of substance, making it hard for his little girl to relate to others face-to-face and one-on-one. I could only offer him a crooked grin, since arguing with one's boss isn't conducive to a harmonious work environment. Ten minutes earlier I made plans via instant messenging to meet up with Kristen, who I met on the internet, to sit and chat at a coffee shop in West Hollywood, followed by Italian at Café Med on the Sunset Strip. I'm unaware of any sort of human disconnect occurring from networking software and internet use; it was always a way to connect, for me. Plus, my boss' daughter plays drums in a band and is active in sports, so I kept thinking she must be doing better at communicating to her peers than a lot of kids. Her activities require teamwork. Basketball requires an enormous amount of nonverbal communication, an understanding of the nuances of body language. Composing songs with a band demands a high level of creative communication, an almost empathic understanding of what fellow musicians are thinking and feeling. I really just wanted to make him feel better by pointing these things out, but he was pretty set in his worry. He's a parent; it's his job to worry about kids these days.

This brings me back to Catalina, where my best friends in the entire world often sought out quiet time alone to recharge from all the togetherness. Some of that time included talking to other people on discussion boards and via instant messenger, even though we were sitting right next to each other on the couch. I'm afraid I might be painting a picture of people who couldn't connect unless there was an electronic buffer between them, which really isn't true. It might not seem so silly if everyone grabbed books, or knit in front of a movie on a lazy afternoon. Our rental house was filled with these alone-time activities as well.

The laptops closed for community meals and island exploration. Making Thanksgiving dinner for eight involves a high degree of cooperation, or we'd all be gnawing at raw turkey on the dining room floor like jackals. Lori was in the kitchen making a roux and checking the temperature of the bird. Anything that involves mechanics is Lori's job, from assembling IKEA furniture to figuring out how long it takes twelve pounds of poultry to cook. Sara and I set the table and made salad. Lee and ita kept mimosas flowing, Paula nuked the frozen corn, and Kat made frequent trips to the island's wee grocery store for the things we forgot to buy, while sauteing green beans and almonds. I have no idea how she did both at the same time; I suspect sorcery. We managed to do all of this without tripping over each other, while drinking and laughing and gossiping about each ourselves and other people.

When I found myself slowing down, right before crankiness set in, I excused myself and went for a walk down to the grocery. I picked up markers, a pad of paper, Tootsie Pops, and fancy napkins. I wandered into the florist shop and picked up bunches of lilies and greens. My energy levels ticked back up while I studied floral arrangements in the refrigerator, brushing the shop owner's sales pitches aside and thinking about the dining room table back at the rental.

I returned with some bunches of fresh flowers, and Lori rinsed out empty bottles of champagne and Dos Equis for my cheap centerpiece arrangement of booze and lilies. Table settings were crudely fashioned paper napkin rings with a Tootsie Pop holding them together. We stuffed ourselves silly and then did what all families do after Thanksgiving; we found comfortable spots to snooze away the tryptophan.

Communal dining was every day. For breakfast, ita and Lori would serve us homemade pancakes, cinnamon rolls, bacon, and sausage. Sara and Paula would wash the dishes together, and no one ever put the kettle on without asking who else wanted a cup of tea. We all napped, went for walks together and alone, shared caramel apples, went wading into the freezing Catalina water, snorkeled, purchased souvenirs, and napped some more. Marathon games of Scrabble were played with Paula and ita, who are both so frighteningly competitive it's hard to lose to either one of them without feeling like they are imagining your head on a spike as a warning to all who would be foolish enough to challenge them. I usually feel less like I lost a game, and more like the Roman army has conquered my people and my land when I play games with either of them.

There was a small incident with the unlocked-pantry-rifle in which Lori and ita practiced aiming and how to disarm someone pointing a gun at one's head. I've watched too many cautionary cheap made-for-TV movies about how "There's no such thing as an unloaded gun," and imagined having to call ita's mom in Jamaica and explain how we managed to murder her daughter on our vacation. "You see, Dr. ita's mom, guns don't kill people, Lori kills people." Thankfully, they got bored and put the gun away before they could fulfill the promise of the made-for-TV movie.

Throughout the weekend, even with laptops and places to nap, I'd look up to find someone pulling on a jacket and announce that she was going for a walk while the door was closing shut behind her.

Ever since I can remember, I would find a place to hide and be by myself at family gatherings. My mom would be furious to find me locked in my room with a book. To her, it's the rudest thing ever. My father and grandfather would escape to the garage and smoke cigars in silence, while the women would holler and cackle in the dining room. It was okay for my dad and grandfather to hide in the garage, I guess, because they're men, and so the women just thought them odd creatures anyway. My mom thought they were bonding or something, but really, they were escaping the din of togetherness.

My dad is an introvert who immediately turned my bedroom into his own personal shrine to television when I moved out of the house. My mom is an extrovert who thrives on company. Her own Pavlovian response to the doorbell's ring is to put the kettle on for company. Mine is to hide under the bed and hope everyone leaves me be. I can't even be in a mall at Christmas without feeling irate in less than five minutes due to too many people. My introverted self says a prayer of thanks to Amazon.com and 1-800-Flowers.com for their very existence. I never have to struggle with thousands of strangers in a mall ever again. They're like vampires, sucking the life from me by walking too slowly and arguing with cashiers about expired coupons.

Those family gatherings would have been so much easier if I could have taken fifteen-minute breathers. Smoking covers that, now. I just excuse myself to stand out on the porch, indulging my filthy habit while recharging for the next round of "The Beatrice Who Fucked Up the Most Since the Last Holiday Gathering." If I busted out a laptop at the table, my mom would go apoplectic.

In Catalina, no one had to explain their reasons for escapism. It was an unspoken understanding that we were recuperating. It wasn't a statement of dislike about anyone in the rental, since we were all so comfortable with our company that the rifle in the pantry would rest forgotten, instead of being the subject of fantasy executions of our fellow rental residents.

We were all just behaving as the introverted creatures we are, except for Paula, who soaked up the energy of being together even if together was hip to hip on the couch cuddling warm iBooks on our laps.

My friends and I have started making plans for our next Thanksgiving. Kat made a deposit on a cabin in Big Bear. Amenities include pool table, hot tub, washer/dryer, DVD players, cable television, and of course, free wireless internet.

About the Author

When Allyson Beatrice isn't watching television, she's writing about it on the internet. Raised on a steady programming diet of the Saturday Creature Double Feature, *Good Times* reruns, and ABC After School Specials, Ms. Beatrice's schoolgirl crush on scripted programming developed in her mid-twenties into an unhealthy love affair with the cult show *Buffy the Vampire Slayer*. She sought out conversation with other television junkies on message boards and found a sense of family among the strangers logging onto sites to pledge allegiance to the little blonde girl with the big stake.

Allyson is the cofounder of EMA, an event-planning and consulting company that specializes in internet community events, fan gatherings, and entertainment industry events. She lives in Los Angeles with her paranoid cat Ruby.